Deinstitutionalization and Community Living in Sweden and Japan

Author:
Hiroshi Katoda

Translator:
Hirano Catharine Jane

Back-up translator:
Boregren-Matsui Yoshiko

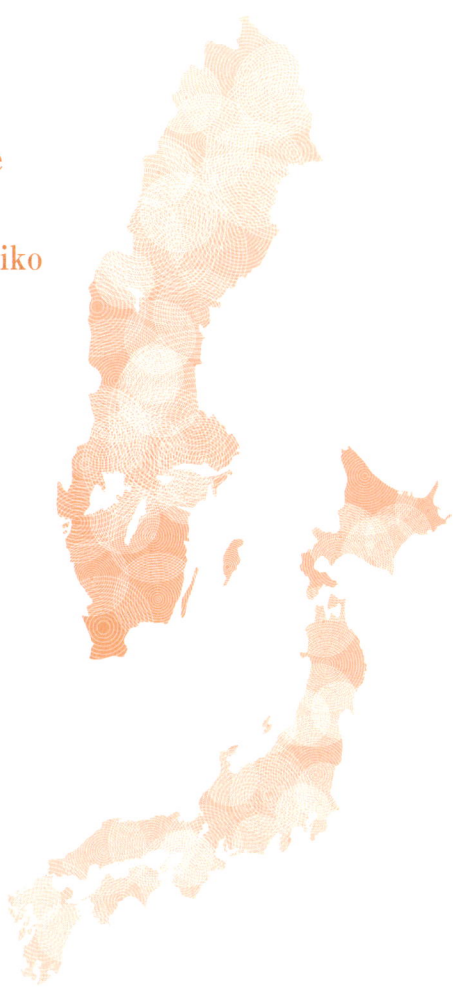

©Hiroshi Katoda, February 28, 2014

Gendaishokan Publishing Co., Ltd.
3-2-5 Iidabashi Chiyoda-ku, Tokyo
102-0072 Japan
Tel:+81-(0)3-3221-1321／Fax:+81-(0)3-3262-5906
ISBN978-4-7684-3530-4

Printing Office : Hirakawakogyosha/Tokoinsatsusho, Tokyo
Binder : Yajimaseihon, Tokyo

Table of Contents

Preface ··· *3*

Chapter 1 The Normalization Principle, Deinstitutionalization and Community Living ··· *15*

    Section 1 Discussion of the Normalization Principle in 1946   *16*
    Section 2 Development of the Normalization Principle after 1946   *18*
    Section 3 The Normalization Principle as an Ideology for Securing Human Rights and Inclusion   *20*
    Section 4 The Normalization Principle, Deinstitutionalization and Community Living in Sweden after 1980   *23*

Chapter 2 Deinstitutionalization and Community Living in Sweden ··· *34*

    Section 1 Legislation of the Normalization Principle and Deinstitutionalization and Community Living   *34*
    Section 2 The Dissolution of Carlslund and Deinstitutionalization Policies in Sweden   *42*

Chapter 3 Deinstitutionalization and Community Living in Japan ··· *57*

    Section 1 Social Welfare Policies for the Disabled and Deinstitutionalization and Community Living in Japan   *57*
    Section 2 The State of Deinstitutionalization and Community Living in Japan   *82*

Chapter 4 The State of Deinstitutionalization and Community Living and Issues in Sweden and Japan — From the Perspective of an Interview Survey of Former Institution Residents ··· *106*

Section 1 Outline of the Interview Survey of Former Institution Residents in
          Sweden and Japan   *107*
Section 2 Concerning the (Former) Institutions Surveyed   *110*
Section 3 Results of the Comparison of Deinstitutionalization and Community
          Living in Sweden and Japan   *112*
Section 4 Factors that Impacted the Results of the Comparison of
          Deinstitutionalization and Community Living in the Two Countries   *125*

Chapter 5 The Realization of the Normalization Principle and Deinstitutionalization
          and Community Living ··· *134*

Section 1 What the Study Results Revealed   *134*
Section 2 Deinstitutionalization and Community Living to Meet Individual
          Needs   *139*

Afterword ·· *155*

Appendix Interview Guides used in the interview surveys in Sweden and Japan in
          Chapter 4 ·· *163*

Preface

1. On Writing the Preface

While aware that such content is highly unusual for a preface, there is one event which I feel compelled to record: the Great East Japan Earthquake and Tsunami which occurred on March 11, 2011. This catastrophe left almost 20,000 dead and missing and triggered meltdowns and explosions in three nuclear reactors at the Fukushima Daiichi plant that released radioactive material into the atmosphere. This catastrophe, unprecedented not only in its scale but also in its combination of natural and manmade disasters, occurred just as I was formulating the concept for this publication, and it brought my pen to an abrupt halt. Every year I travel to Sweden—but not that year. Swedish friends and colleagues sent emails and letters, asking after me and expressing their condolences. Although I had promised to see them all again in September 2011, I had no choice but to abandon this plan. Why? Because my family home was located in the disaster area. It took two weeks to confirm that my family had survived, and, while we were fortunate that the house was still standing, it had tilted on its foundation, a stone wall had collapsed, and ceiling boards had fallen. For some time after the disaster, frequent aftershocks shook the area on a daily basis, and the distress deeply impacted the mental state of my parents and siblings. A year and a half have passed since then but the effects of the earthquake, tsunami and nuclear accident are still immense, and the problems they created remain unresolved.

What were we doing at 14:46 March 11, 2011? I am sure that some immediately went to the afflicted areas to help, and some prayed desperately for the safety of the survivors and a quick recovery for the whole region. I was one of countless people stranded at work, unable to return home because all transportation shut down. I spent many long days in anguish, worrying about my family and friends in Sendai and all the people I knew in the afflicted region, unable travel to the region for various reasons. Still, I did what I could, sending funds and helping to procure goods. Piece by piece, I learned that not just my family but also many friends and acquaintances had suffered damage to their homes, some irreparable, and that people I knew who had lived along the coast had been swept away by the tsunami. Slowly, the mass media revealed the enormity of the situation—the scarcity of goods, the severing of lifelines and of community ties, the isolation of some and the mass evacuation of others, the incapacity of the government administration, radioactive contamination, and the destruction of cities and towns and the natural environment.

I and my colleagues を have continued to visit the disaster areas repeatedly — sometimes with coworkers, sometimes with students, sometimes as members of a family directly impacted by the disaster. Each time we go, we reel with shock at the reality of the situation. Our feet falter, our knees tremble, frustration and powerlessness weigh down our hearts. But time moves on inexorably. We must convey this experience to succeeding generations lest it be forgotten. For this reason I feel that, even if the content differs, now is precisely the time to superimpose this publication's theme of coexistence on the types of support extended to the disaster areas and to explore what we can do now and in the future.

2. Reflecting Once Again on What Occurred in the Disaster Areas

A year has passed since the Great East Japan Earthquake and Tsunami. Drawing from documents and personal experiences, I record here what happened in the disaster areas during that year looking first at (1) March 11, the day of the disaster, followed by (2) events from March 12 to the present.

(1) March 11, the Day of the Disaster

"One person dropped her one-year-old off at her parents' home while she went to work. Her family was swept away, house and all, by the tsunami. Only she survived—because she was at work." "I went to my wife's kindergarten but no one was there. I heard that my wife had taken refuge in the junior high school, and that's where I found her. Apparently, she and the children had walked there when they evacuated. Many children who had been picked up by their parents didn't survive... Elderly people were incontinent, and so many people were in a miserable state." "One of my colleagues died. He was directing the users so that they could escape. Just as he finished, the tsunami came and he was washed away." (Yasuko Sugita, 2012)

"On the day of the disaster, after the big quake, we didn't know what was going on. We learned that a tsunami was coming from one of the staff who happened to see a digital news transmission on his cellphone ... We started driving the users to safety, going back and forth. Somehow we managed to get everyone out before the tsunami hit, so all the users and staff were saved... While we were escaping, the staff members had the foresight to bring the users' jackets. March is still cold. If we had escaped without warm clothes, I don't think they would have survived the night..." "(All the users escaped but) one of the staff members who went back to retrieve something was washed away by the tsunami." (Sanae Ando et al, 2012)

(2) Events from March 12 to the Present
1) Conditions Immediately After the Disaster

"There wasn't enough space in the shelters. People who saw the lights on at our facility for the disabled started pouring in... Our disaster rations were quickly exhausted because we were feeding people from the community as well." "At the day service center... we couldn't contact the users' families, so we arranged for them to stay the night. After that, those who had places to return to were sent home. As for those who had nowhere to go, it was really hard trying to figure out how to help their families. All the staff got involved, helping to clear homes of rubble, etc. We worked together to make a place for each user to return to... Residential facilities and day care facilities were filled to two or three times their capacity with people from the community as well as people from group homes and care homes." (Sugita, 2012)

2) Conditions in the Shelters

"We went to the shelter after the disaster but it was so crowded. There was no place to even stand and no way people could use the toilet under such conditions, so we returned to the office... No provisions had been made for extra toilets in an emergency...These are the problems...No shelters for people with special needs, and no space set aside in regular disaster shelters for the weak and vulnerable... The shelters (including temporary housing) are not barrier free...Communication of information [is very poor]." (Makoto Saito, 2012)

The same situation in different forms was evident in the 1995 Great Hanshin-Awaji Earthquake and the 2004 Chuetsu Earthquake, as described below.

"There were many problems in the shelters... they were not designed for living in... the environment was extremely harsh for people with disabilities and the elderly. People had to go too long without privacy. Women and children were not protected from sexual violence. There is a pressing need for psychological care at an early stage." "From calls to telephone counseling centers for women, [it was clear that] many women are suffering from violence perpetrated by husbands and boyfriends as well as from loneliness and powerlessness..." (Reiko Masai, 2005)

3) Disaster Trauma

"The impact of the disaster remains very deep in ways that aren't visible. For example, some of the staff members lost their family and some of the users are still traumatized by what they experienced..." (Ando, 2012)

4) Situation for the Disabled and Foreigners Living in the Community in the Disaster Areas

"Home caregivers and sign language interpreters were also victims of the disaster. They had to send out an SOS announcing a crisis in supports for the disabled who were living independently... The disabled who left the shelter are living in damaged homes and have become isolated... People with mental illness who were living in the community were robbed of the infrastructure required to maintain daily life and of their relationships with other people. Some have been forced to return to hospitals. As for homes rented from private owners... the need for renovations is an obstacle for persons with severe disabilities. Providing essential information to people with visual and hearing impairments is also an issue." (Welfare and Labor Editing Committee, 2012)

"Many foreigners were also affected by this massive disaster. According to the Ntional Police Agency, 29 foreigners lost their lives as of 27 June, 2011, of which nealy 70%, 20 people died in Miyagi. Studies on the behavior of foreigners immediately following the earthquake showed that, in addition to luck, Japanese language ability, neighborhood relationships, and disaster awareness were among the factors that determined whether they lived or died." (Editorial Office, Kahoku Shimpo Publishing Co., 2012)

Various reports revealed other issues. "The disabled have to move from one shelter to another"; "the disabled are forced to shelter in their cars because there is no room in the official shelters"; "people with disabilities are forced to live at home"; "residential facilities for the disabled are overcrowded with refugees (and, for that matter, what does it mean that the general public is taking shelter in residential facilities instead of community shelters?)"; "people with disabilities are isolated after evacuation or relocation". Moreover, people with disabilities suffered twice as many casualties as ordinary people. Reports on community living also made it clear that the disabled were "confined" in their rooms. Such accounts are corroborated by the following report:

"When we were providing support, I sensed discrimination against people with disabilities. The community was already rather closed, and it appears that people with disabilities were not accepted. Prior to the disaster, they were treated as a nuisance by their neighbors. They were not seen as human beings and were unable to get the services they needed. At the time of the disaster, they weren't able to get to the shelters, and if they couldn't get to places that distributed relief supplies on their own, they had nothing. This situation demonstrates a pressing need to improve the support system and raise awareness of disabilities." (Tadahiro Iriya, 2012)

Nor should we overlook those things that the victims themselves identified as issues with the aid provided. "The thing that made me angriest was probably the attitude of the social workers sent from other prefectures to help. What we needed most was help clearing out the debris and mud from the day service users' homes, but they told us that they were sent here as professional social workers, not to help with cleaning up. This made me furious because it was so obvious that what they offered was not what we needed at that time." (Sugita, 2012)

3. Lessons Learned about How to Respond in Times of Disaster

Despite the situation described above and the inherent problems of disaster assistance, many organizations collaboratively or independently assessed the situation in the extensive region affected, dispatched supporters quickly into the field, and fully exploited their existing networks to procure and deliver necessary supplies to victims, secure shelter suited to the victims' needs, and provide continuing support. These organizations included the Japan Council on Independent Living Centers (JIL), Yumekaze Fund, the Japan Disability Forum (JDF), the Japan National Assembly of Disabled People's International (DPI), Kyodoren, Tsunagu Project for People with Disabilities in the Disaster Areas, the National Association for Supported Living for the Disabled (Support-ken), Inclusion Japan, the Japanese Association on Intellectual Disability, the Center for Multicultural Information and Assistance, and the Women's Network for the East Japan Disaster (Rise Together). There were also many support groups that delegated tasks among themselves so that they could work more efficiently, catching those who had fallen through the cracks and connecting them to assistance. All of these organizations and groups shared certain common elements in their approach and philosophy. They believed that the vulnerable must not become isolated or shunted from place to place but rather should be assured a stable and comfortable refuge; they addressed the problems of the vulnerable in their recovery plans, including the fact that some missed out on available supports; they provided assistance from the perspective of the vulnerable; and they believed in the need to build a community in which everyone can live a normal life with the supports they need.

We must recognize, however, that prejudice, discrimination and exclusion of the particularly vulnerable, which existed prior to the disaster, were also manifested in the shelters and in temporary housing units after the disaster. In addition, the northeast coast of Japan where the disaster occurred is a remote and predominantly rural region where traditional customs and local culture prevail. People there are bound by strong ties. On

Oshima, an island in Kessenuma, Miyagi prefecture, which I visit occasionally, three-generation families retain the custom of sitting down for meals together and a traditional culture that is both enviable and unimaginable to most people living in urban areas. At times, the islanders have excluded outsiders, maintaining strong bonds among local residents and developing a distinctive local culture. As I listened to disaster victims during my visits, I felt I finally understood what had driven me to leave my own rural community and head for the city. I also realized that many people in the disaster areas still treasure the relationships they have cultivated for so many years. Their ties to local culture and neighbors served as a psychological anchor, yet many have been irretrievably broken, severed, and scattered to the point of no return.

I will never forget one elderly woman I met in March 2012 in Nobiru, Higashimatsushima City in Miyagi prefecture. At over seventy years of age, she had lost her husband and one child in the tsunami. She was now living with her remaining son and his family in a temporary housing unit. Although she acted cheerful, she was actually quite depressed and thought of her missing family members daily. A year had passed, but she was unable to fill the empty space inside (and is probably still unable to do so). When I left, I said, "Please fill that hole in your heart soon." "You fill it!" she cried as she threw her arms around me. I was paralyzed by the pain and intense grief she felt. This incident made me very aware that recovery and reconstruction is meaningless if we do not fill the gaping holes the disaster has left in each person's heart.

4. Deinstitutionalization and Denuclearization

On January 15, 2012, I published a Japanese translation of *From Institutional Life to Community Participation: Ideas and Realities Concerning Support to Persons with Intellectual Disability* (co-translated by Mizuho Dahl-Koseki; originally published by Acta Universitatis Upsaliensis, Uppsala Studies in Education 99, Uppsala 2002). The author was Kent Ericsson (hereinafter referred to as Kent) from the Faculty of Educational Sciences, Uppsala University. This work represents Kent's doctoral thesis into which he poured tremendous energy and his love for the residents, which as strong as his love for his own family.

In the late 1970s, the county of Stockholm decided to close down the residential institution known as Carlslund and launched a project to prepare for the systematic relocation of its many residents to the community. It was Kent who was appointed to serve as the project's representative. Through this work, he met many residents living in Carlslund and, through listening to what they had to say, was inspired to help them realize their dream of a life outside the institution. He devoted his efforts to paving the way for them to live in the community as participating members of society. The impact of these efforts can be found in the words "community participation" which he used in the title of his treatise. As Section 1 of Chapter 2 presents a detailed summary of his treatise, I will limit myself here to recording the connection between radiation contamination and Kent's illness and subsequent death.

I stayed in Uppsala for one year from April 2008 to March 2009 during which time, as a joint researcher with Kent and his wife, I studied the various processes that led from the establishment of residential institutions in Sweden to their dissolution and closure. This book is one of the fruits of that research. I and my wife became close friends with the Ericssons. Not only did we conduct surveys together, but the Ericssons also invited us on a tour of historical properties related to Swedish welfare that still remain in the vicinity of Uppsala. I have wonderful memories from that year. During the course of our friendship, I learned that he had leukemia and did not have much longer to live. This knowledge made our friendship over that year even more meaningful.

On April 22, 2009, soon after I returned to Japan, I received an urgent message from Sweden. It was from Kent's beloved daughter. She gave me the sad news that Kent had passed away. Unfortunately, I could not attend the funeral due to work commitments but I sent flowers from Japan and on September 28, 2009, I was able to visit his grave and place flowers there. His death was a great loss. At 65 years of age, he was still young. It fills me with regret to think how much he could have contributed to deinstitutionalization and community living in the international field. His family often said that they believed his leukemia was caused by exposure to radioactive contamination from the 1986 Chernobyl nuclear accident. "He was forced to live with the fear of death because of Chernobyl," they told me. Kent demonstrated through his own life the horror of radioactive contamination from the Fukushima nuclear explosion caused by the Great East Japan Earthquake and Tsunami. He taught us that we do not need nuclear power generation in this world and left us with the mission of confronting the two issues he wrote so much about—deinstitutionalization and denuclearization.

5. Thoughts on Composing this Book

(1) The Normalization Principle and Recovery and Reconstruction of the Disaster Areas

The aim of the normalization principle is to make it possible for everyone to live and work together in the community. If this concept is useful for protecting the rights of people with disabilities (and particularly those with intellectual disabilities who are always relegated to the bottom rung of society and subjected to prejudice and discrimination), if it is useful for the recovery of human dignity, then we must make it a social principle for combatting all forms of discrimination and prejudice and apply it to measures for reconstruction and recovery in every area affected by the natural and nuclear disaster. To do this, we must address the issue of how to use the normalization principle effectively. With this consideration in mind, I would like to turn to the main subject of this work.

(2) Five Issues

The number of studies and surveys on relocation has increased noticeably since October 2004, when the Ministry of Health, Labour and Welfare presented its plan for relocation in the community in its Grand Design (Draft) and other documents. The actual ratio of people being relocated in the field (residential institutions), however, is still low and the pace has been very slow. Measures to support community living also remain inadequate. With the enactment of the Services and Supports for Persons with Disabilities Act in April 2006 and the Comprehensive Support for Persons with Disabilities Act in June 2012, the ratio of people being relocated from institutions to the community is increasing and support systems for community living are gradually being put into place. Japan's approach, however, consists of retaining residential institutions even while relocating the disabled to the community, and thus it differs dramatically from that in advanced welfare states in places like Scandinavia where the expressed aim of deinstitutionalization is to abolish institutions. Perhaps this situation arises from the difference between the normalization principle, which is based on equality, and the family-centered classic Japanese style of welfare (culture) and Japan's new liberalist society and sociopolitical framework, which are based on the principle of competition. If we truly wish to foster the normalization principle in Japan, which was introduced in the Amendment to the Eight Welfare-Related Laws in 1990, we must return to the fundamental question of "what is normalization?" and work towards its concrete realization. As Bengt Nirje, the father of the normalization concept, recorded in his comprehensive work The Normalization Principle Papers, "In future, residential institutions will become obsolete and disappear (Bengt Nirje, 1992, p.7)." It was for that purpose that he "incorporated" the normalization principle.

The aim of this book is to examine the impact that the differences in the understanding of the normalization principle between Japan and Sweden has had on the creation of social mechanisms, and, on that basis, to explore our thesis in order to clarify the following:

Issue 1: The normalization principle as a basic social welfare principle and its impact on deinstitutionalization and community living.

Issue 2: Sweden's approach to deinstitutionalization and community living, which was based on its adoption of the normalization principle in policy implementation, and how it overcame various problems that arose.

Issue 3: The reality of and issues in deinstitutionalization and community living in Japan.

Issue 4: The issues in deinstitutionalization and community living in Japan as seen through a comparison between Sweden and Japan.

Issue 5: The conditions required for Japan to achieve deinstitutionalization and community living.

Each of the above issues will be thoroughly examined and explored in separate chapters (Chapter 1, issue 1, Chapter 2, issue 2, Chapter 3, issue 3, Chapter 4, issue 4, and Chapter 5, issue 5). The final chapter will also explore the need for the social realization of the normalization principle and how to confront prejudice and discrimination, as well as how to confront natural and manmade disasters such as a major earthquake and a nuclear accident.

This book represents the research results for the "Study on Deinstitutionalization and the Construction of a Community Living Support System" (20330126; study representative: Hiroshi Katoda) conducted under a Grant-in-Aid for Scientific Research (Basic Research (B)) from the Japan Society for the Promotion of Science (JSPS). Because the study focused on Sweden and Japan, the title chosen was "Deinstitutionalization and Community Living in Sweden and Japan".

References and Sources

1. Ando, Sanae, et al. (2012). *Hito x joho =∞ imakoso tsunagaro, hisaichito! (People & Information= ∞Let's connect now with the disaster area!).* Rikkyo University College of Community and Human Services *Hito x joho =∞* (People & Information= ∞). Activity Report Editing Committee.
2. Inoue, Kimidori (2011). *Watashitachi no shinsai monogatari (Our Tale of the Disaster).* Shuei Inc.
3. Iriya, Tadahiro (2012). "Hisaichi shogaisha senta kamaishi de no shienkatsudo wo okonatte" (Support Activities in Kamaishi Center for the Disabled in the Disaster Area). In *SSKS warera jishin no koe (SSKS Our Own Voice)* Vol. 5431, p. 2.
4. Kahoku Newspaper Editorial Bureau (2012). *Futatabi tachiagaru! Kahoku shimbun, higashinihon daishinsai no kiroku (We Will Rise Again! Kahoku Newspaper's Journal of the Great East Japan Earthquake and Tsunami).* Kahoku Newspaper.
5. Saito, Makoto (2011). "Daishinsai ni okeru saigaijakusha shien hokoku" (Report on Supporting the Vulnerable in a Major Disaster). In *Rezami* Vol. 133, Issue 9094, p. 9. KSKP Kyodoren.
6. Suganuma, Takashi (2011). "Shisutemikku risuku to atarashii kyodo – daishinsai wo keiken shite" (Systemic Risk and New Collaboration – From Experiencing a Great Disaster). In

Shakai Fukushi Nyusu (Social Welfare News), Vol. 33, pp. 1-2. Rikkyo University Institute of Social Welfare.
7. Sugita, Yasuko (2012). "Hisaisha ni manabu" (Learning from Disaster Victims). In *Fukushi Bunka Kenkyu (Human Welfare and Culture Studies)*, Vol. 21, pp. 26-32. Japanese Society for the Study of Human Welfare and Culture.
8. Social Welfare and Labor Editorial Committee (2011). "Higashi nihon daishinsai shogaisha shien apiru" (An Appeal for Support for Disabled Victims of the Great East Japan Earthquake and Tsunami). In *Kikan Fukushirodo (Social Welfare and Labor Quarterly)*, Vol. 131, pp. 8-9.
9. Masai, Reiko (2005). "Bosai ni josei no shiten wo!" (Let's Hear Women's Perspectives on Disaster Prevention!). In *Niigataken Chuetsu jishin taisaku ni okeru 'josei no shiten' no hanei ni tsuite –Hanshin awaji daishinsai no jirei kenkyu kara (Concerning Women's Perspectives on Measures for the Niigata-Chuetsu Earthquake: From Case Studies on the Great Hanshin-Awaji Earthquake)*. Kobe Municipal Gender Equality Bureau.
10. Nirje, Bengt (1992). *The Normalization Principle Papers*. Uppsala University: Reprocentralen HSC, p.7.

Chapter 1
The Normalization Principle, Deinstitutionalization and Community Living

I used to work in a residential institution when such institutions were in their heyday. It therefore warms my heart to see such statements as these on the websites of many social services organizations:

> Normalization is our goal. We aim to make sure that all can enjoy the same standard of life, regardless of whether they have disabilities or not. We seek to establish the legal foundation for the respect and support of human dignity, to improve the living environment and to promote participation in society.[1]

> We are convinced that the essence (aim) of our work 'is the creation of a society that recognizes diverse values.' In the simplest Japanese, the idea of normalization essentially means that 'a society with diverse kinds of people is a truly healthy society.' Perhaps through supporting people with disabilities to live in the community we are really proclaiming to all, 'Recognize and celebrate who you are!'[2]

The shift demonstrated by these statements proves that the normalization principle is indeed helping us to protect civil rights and that our society is advancing towards the concrete realization of normalization. Happy to be witnessing the advent of this era, I would like to devote this chapter to exploring the origins and development of the normalization principle, which has now firmly penetrated the field of social welfare services, as well as its impact on deinstitutionalization and community living and its future directions.[3]

Section 1 Discussion of the Normalization Principle in 1946

I have already drawn attention in previous papers[4] to the debate concerning the normalization principle which took place in Sweden during the mid-1940s. My accounts were based on papers[5] by Kent Ericsson published in 1985, 1986, 1992 and 2000, in which he introduced the Report of the Committee on Employment for the Partially Ablebodied published by Sweden's Ministry of Health and Social Affairs in 1946 (hereunder referred to as "the Committee" and "the Report"), and other related reports.[6]

The Committee was established in 1943 as an advisory body under the jurisdiction of Sweden's Ministry of Health and Social Affairs to promote social welfare reform, and it consisted of nine members including persons with disabilities who were recommended for this post by organizations for the disabled. Prerequisite to the discussions was the understanding that all people are of equal value and that an individual's basic social rights should be viewed not as a personal issue but rather as an issue of an individual member of society[7], and the Committee began its investigation with the belief that this understanding must form the guiding principle of democracy. The Committee's founding objective also demonstrates that it sought to establish the foundation for Sweden's current system of social services for the disabled.

In the Committee's 1946 Report, the term "normalization" appears only once in the following passage, yet this makes the document precious evidence that the principle of normalization was already being earnestly discussed in the mid-1940s.

> In full accordance with the ambitions of our work for social progress, it is apparent to this committee for the partially able-bodied, that the agreed upon principle is *that the partially able-bodied to as great an extent as possible be included in the ordinary system of social services which are being developed in our country*. It follows therefore, as a working hypothesis, that no special solution outside the general framework should be suggested, before the applicability of the general solution, even for these categories, be tried and before it has been proved

that the general organization cannot within reason be adjusted for this, in certain respects, special clientele.

It is hardly necessary to emphasize that this, even for the partially able-bodied themselves, must be seen as a basic right as a citizen; it is entirely in keeping with the very essence of democracy that equal human value and equal rights are put in the foreground. The institutions of society must be adapted in order to justly and if possible according to the circumstances, include all individuals, irrespective of which category they belong regarding physical ability, intellectual capacity, economic resources etc. To exclude certain categories from the general plan and agree on special arrangements for them naturally cannot always be avoided, but it must be the exception, not the rule. Psychologically this "normalization" of conditions of life, education, employment exchange, etc. of the partially able-bodied must be a great achievement.[8]

The next time the normalization principle was publicly addressed was in the 1949 Ministry of Health and Social Affairs report "The Problem of the Partially Ablebodied."[9] The report stated that:

The normalization principle, as proposed by the committee, implies, amongst other things, that special institutions for the partially able-bodied, concerning education, schooling, etc. should be an exception, not the rule. This means that ... people who are blind participate in the same learning circles as people who can see.[10]

The normalization principle was further mentioned in the 1951 Report of the Committee of Inquiry on the Care of the Feebleminded[11] published in 1955. Here I would like to quote from Ericsson's paper of 2002 in which he introduced this report:

The 1951 Committee on the care of the feebleminded had a mandate to "... dissociate itself from so-called institutional thinking" (citation from 1951 års sinnesslövårdsutredning 1952, p.15)[12] and instead to suggest open forms of care for persons with an intellectual disability. In its report, the enquiry presented an analysis on the subject (1951 års sinnesslövårdsutredning 1955) and in an appendix, Bergh (1955) presented the normalization principle as it had been formulated by the Committee for the partially able-bodied, as well as a proposal for measures which would facilitate the procurement of employment for partially able-bodied persons. Bergh who wrote this appendix was most active in advocating the normalization principle in the work to assist persons with a disability to get employment.[13]

As shown here, it is possible to clearly identify references to the normalization principle in at least these three reports from the Ministry of Health and Social Affairs published in 1946, 1949 and 1955, and the principle was certainly the subject of debate. Unfortunately, however, it is impossible to determine the depth to which the subject was discussed because the details are not recorded in these reports.

As can be seen from the above, the term "normalization principle" is used in the Report of the Committee for partially able-bodied persons, and there is at least no doubt that the content indicated that people with disabilities should be assured the same social services guaranteed to the general public and should enjoy the same rights as members of society.

Section 2 Development of the Normalization Principle after 1946

After 1946, a new development in the normalization principle occurred in Denmark, inspired by the actions of the Danish association for parents of the mentally retarded. In response to a letter of request from that association, the Danish Ministry of Social Welfare established a committee of inquiry on social services issues in 1953. Nils Erik Bank-Mikkelsen was in charge of the committee's executive office. When compiling the committee's report, he focused on the actions of the aforementioned Swedish Ministry of Health and Social Affairs' committee for partially able-bodied persons, and particularly on the principle of normalization that the committee was discussing. Concerning Bank-Mikkelsen's actions at this time, Ericsson writes as follows:

> Much of his original work was formulated during visits to Sweden. His partner and colleague was Nordfors, an educationalist who had been one of the experts in the 1951 Committee. A great deal of the preparatory work prior to the Danish legislation of 1959 was carried out by Bank-Mikkelsen and Nordfors in Upplands-Väsby (the municipality where Carlslund residential home was situated).[14]

Having learned much from the discussions of the normalization principle recorded in the series of reports for the Swedish Ministry of Health and Social Affairs, Bank-Mikkelsen incorporated considerable content related to the principle in his report for the Danish committee. The 1959 Act Concerning the Care of the Mentally Retarded[15] was drafted on the basis of this report, and the related documents contain many statements that intimate the concept of normalization.[16] Bank-Mikkelsen, who dedicated himself to formulating this legislation, came to be known in the social welfare field as one of those who defined and developed the normalization principle.

The statements on normalization in the documents for the Danish Act Concerning the Care of the Mentally Retarded were reintroduced to Sweden as an approach for reforming contemporary social conditions, and in 1967, the Act on Special Services for the Mentally Retarded,[17] which incorporated the normalization principle, was enacted. This legislation established an education system for all school-age children, regardless of disabilities, and provided for qualitative improvements in the living environment by reviewing the institution-centered approach to care and introducing alternatives in the form of group homes, the small group system, and personal care programs. This represented a major shift from "care" to "support", a new concept in the field of social services for people with intellectual disabilities.

From the latter half of the 1960s, Bank-Mikkelsen and Bengt Nirje collaborated at Scandinavian and other international conferences for the dissemination of the normalization principle, a fact attested to in Nirje's memorandum.[18] In this, Nirje records that Karl

Grunewald, who provided administrative support to Swedish disability welfare, was also involved in the drafting of the 1967 Act on special services for some mentally retardet (SFS 1967:940).

Through actual experience with such policies for the disabled in Denmark and Sweden, and through further inquiry into the same, as well as through Nirje's treatise (1969)[19], a systematic and valuable framework for the normalization principle began to emerge. Until then, Wolf Wolfensberger notes, virtually no one had heard of the term "normalization".[20]

Because Nirje's "principle of normalization" identified essential human rights in concrete and simple terms, it quickly gained the attention of people involved in the social welfare field worldwide. In 1972, Wolfensburger introduced his own culture-specific principle of normalization[21] in order to spread the principle to countries with different cultures. The debate concerning whether or not his approach was appropriate drew the interest of many others, and the normalization principle spread rapidly to other countries.

Section 3 The Normalization Principle as an Ideology for Securing Human Rights and Inclusion

In the conclusion of *Changing Patterns in Residential Services for the Mentally Retarded*[22], the report of the President's Committee on Mental Retardation in the United States, Gunnar Dybwad lauds the normalization principle codified by Nirje in 1969.[23]

> Without a doubt, as far as the future of residential (as well as many other) services is concerned, the concept of normalization presented in Nirje's chapter has emerged as the most important one in this book. Developed in Scandinavia where it had long been reflected in the broad network of human welfare services even before the particular term was adopted, this concept is elegant in its simplicity and parsimony. It can be readily understood by everyone, and it has most far-reaching implications in practice.[24]

By "the concept of normalization presented in Nirje's chapter", Dybwad is referring not only to Nirje's definition of "making available to the mentally retarded patterns and conditions of everyday life which are as close as possible to the norms and patterns of mainstream society"[25] but also to the eight well-known features[26] Nirje identified as the basic framework of the principle, namely:

1. to experience a normal rhythm of day for the retarded;
2. to experience a normal routine of life;
3. to experience the normal rhythm of the year, with holidays and family days of personal significance;
4. to have an opportunity to undergo normal developmental experiences of the life cycle;
5. the choices, wishes and desires of the mentally retarded themselves have to be taken into consideration as nearly as possible, and respected;
6. to live in a bisexual world;
7. to apply normal economic standards; and,
8. the standards of the physical facilities, e.g. hospitals, schools, group homes and hostels, and boarding homes, should be the same as those regularly applied in society to the same kind of facilities for ordinary citizens

Nirje also emphasized that the normalization principle "applies to all retarded people, whatever their degree of handicap. Obviously it applies to all other persons with handicaps and to minority groups as well"[27] and that it could be "useful in every society, for all age groups, and can be adapted to individual developments or social changes."[28] Furthermore, the "principle serves as an instrument for determining that which is appropriate, both for raising questions and for finding answers"[29] and as "indicators of proper human programs, and legislation".[30] He also stated that "The principle is useful in every society, can be adapted to social changes and individual developments. So it should serve as a guide for medical, educational, psychological, social and political work."[31] Finally, he declared that the reason he codified the normalization principle was "to demonstrate that institutions in the end were dead ends".[32]

In Bank-Mikkelsen's paper of 1969 we can find the following statement concerning the conceptualization of the normalization principle:

> The purpose of a modern service for the mentally retarded is to "normalize" their lives. For children, normalization means living in their natural surroundings, playing, going to kindergartens and schools, etc. Adults must have the right to leave the home of their parents, to be trained and taught, and to pursue employment. Children as well as adults need leisure time and recreation as part of a normal life. We are trying to integrate the retarded into the community in the best possible way. We help them in making use of their abilities, no matter how limited these may be. The mentally retarded have, along with other human beings, a basic right to receive the most adequate treatment, training, and rehabilitation available, and to be approached in an ethical fashion. To provide the retarded with normal life conditions does not mean that we are oblivious of our duties to offer special care and support. We simply accept them as they are, with their handicaps, and teach them to live with those handicaps. Whatever services and facilities are open to all other citizens must, in principle, also be available to the mentally retarded.[33]

Bank-Mikkelsen further indicates an approach that could be interpreted as the principle of "inclusion".

> The objective of normalization is not to make the mentally retarded "normal"... Normalization is the acceptance of the mentally retarded, along with their disability (regardless of their disability), and to provide them with normal living conditions.[34]

In addition, Bank-Mikkelsen considers the acquisition of civic rights to be extremely important and insists that the mentally retarded should be given the same rights as those of other citizens:

> Let me add simply that normalization means that the mentally retarded have equal status with other people in all aspects of life, including civil rights. Civil rights are the rights to a place to live, to education and to an occupation. Civil rights also mean the right to vote, to marry, to have children and, even if one does not marry or have children, to have a sexual life.[35]

Both Nirje's and Bank-Mikkelsen's principle of normalization represent the ideology of human rights. Perhaps this was the product of the deeply rooted tradition of philanthropy in Scandinavian countries. The normalization principle was widely disseminated to the world through Nirje and Bank-Mikkelsen and became the fundamental concept that ensured basic human rights and indicated the nature of human services.

Section 4   The Normalization Principle, Deinstitutionalization and Community Living in Sweden after 1980

The 1980s witnessed an increase in research and practical measures to improve social welfare services and living environments based on the principle of normalization and the empowerment of self-advocacy organizations. This in turn accelerated the worldwide movement for the realization of the normalization principle. As the principle came to be incorporated in the legislation of various countries and as social barriers were gradually removed, the living conditions of people with disabilities improved, the process of deinstitutionalization advanced, the closure of residential institutions progressed and a wide array of services to support community living emerged.

Once people with disabilities began to live a full life in the community, life in the institutions appeared even more miserable than before. With the guarantee of opportunities for education, employment and leisure in the community, an increasing number of people with disabilities desired to live independently, and the raison d'etre and purpose of residential institutions gradually changed. Public awareness rose to the point where community life without the inclusion of people with disabilities became inconceivable.

In this way, the normalization principle brought about unprecedented developments and social reform in the provision of services to people with disabilities. As a result, today the disabled, regardless of the severity of their disability, live together with other people in the community. In addition, the normalization principle has been adopted as a common ideology for anyone who needs any kind of support from society.

According to Mårten Söder, however, a slightly different movement can be seen in Sweden. Here, I would like to share some excerpts from Söder's commentary in a compilation that represents a posthumous collection of Nirje's manuscripts.[36]

In Sweden, the principle of normalization had great significance in determining the policies for the first group addressed by the principle, namely, the mentally retarded. In the 1970s, the name of this principle was often mentioned in government documents, FUB reports and debates concerning care ideology.[37]

It also had major significance as an indicator for the ideology of staff education in a variety of fields. Subsequently, it increasingly came to be used not only for the care of the mentally retarded but also as a goal for disability policies in general. At the end of the 1980s, the degree to which the concept was used in documents related to surveys and government policy decreased and was replaced at some point by other concepts.[38]

Around the same period, another national survey was implemented on conditions in schools for the disabled. A special report was prepared ... on this study.[39]

In this report, there is minimal mention of the details of the normalization concept. This was a manifestation of the fact that the concept of normalization was not understood to be as central as the idea of integration in the educational field. The report concluded that the concept of normalization would not be used in the future work to be undertaken because it was too frequently misunderstood.[40]

In fact, the 1980 government report on this study states that:

> Due to the risk of further misunderstandings, and because such misunderstandings affect people's attitudes to the disabled, we, the Integration Committee, have decided to eliminate the term "normalization" from the field of disabilities.[41]

Furthermore, the Support Committee's report (1981) for the establishment of the Act on special services for the mentally retarded and others (SFS 1985:568, enacted in 1986), also expressed doubts about the normalization principle, as follows:

> In the 1970s, the concepts of normalization and integration were used almost exclusively as the guiding principles for support in the field of disabilities. Their initial focus was on individuals, on deciding what should be done for them. Subsequently, the focus shifted away from the individual's disability and the principles adopted the stance that society was in the first place responsible. The principles came to focus on the social environment and phenomena/incidents that cause handikaps.[42]

We can see how the inquiries for policy formulations in the 1980s mark a certain skepticism about the concept of normalization.[43]

When the United Nations codified the basic standards concerning equal opportunities for the disabled, the overall goals were "full participation and equality".[44]

Nor was the concept of normalization mentioned in the inquiry presenting the recommendations, which formed the foundation for disability reforms in 1994. Instead, the general goals are stated as "full participation and equality", "equal human value for everyone", "integrity and self-determination" and "society for all".[45]

We notice that in the final decade of the previous century the objectives of policies for the disabled changed from an emphasis on "integration" and "normalization" to "participation, equality and self-determination".[46]

Söder summarized the reasons[47] that the term "normalization principle" disappeared from Swedish government reports in the 1980s as follows:

1. The aims of the normalization principle did not change; only the term itself changed.
2. The normalization principle was seen from the beginning as referring only to people with intellectual disabilities, and from the 1980s when the debate widened to issues concerning general policies for people with disabilities, the topics of accessibility and participation became the focus rather than "normal" living conditions.
3. Leaders of the empowerment movement who fought for liberation from dependency perceived the normalization principle as having been codified by people who did not have disabilities and therefore they did not show much interest. In fact, they criticized those (experts) who tried to promote normalization.

Adolf Ratzka, the driving force behind the movement for independent living in Sweden and a key figure in the introduction of personal assistance in the Act Concerning Support and Services for Persons with Certain Functional Impairments enacted in 1994, criticized Swedish social welfare policies in his writings[48], advocated "antidiscrimination", "de-medicalization", "deinstitutionalization", and "de-professionalization", and emphasized the importance of "self-management of services" (consumer control). He does not mention the normalization principle in his writings; rather, he criticizes those people (professionals) who promote normalization, declares that the disabled themselves are the real experts, and stresses "gaining control over the personal assistance program"[49] based on "self-determination" and a "high level of funding and consumer control"[50]. Concerning what has been achieved by people with disabilities, Söder, after quoting Michael Oliver, states:

> "The fact that the principle was codified by people who were not disabled means that it is not based on the reality of daily life for people with disabilities."[51]

Just over half a century has passed since the normalization principle was introduced. Even if we set its origins as far back as 1946, only sixty-six years have passed as of 2012. During that time, much debate has surrounded the principle's ideology and interpretations. Although the principle itself must be the same, the differences in understanding based on the perspective or interpretation from which it is viewed have been astounding. In countries such as Sweden, the term "normalization principle" vanished from public documents within three decades due to the influence of the empowerment and independent living movements. In other countries, however, it is considered particularly pertinent in this age of confusion. Japan falls into the latter category. While the policies and directions taken may have varied due to these differences in understanding or interpretation, one thing remains the same: the unwavering determination of those involved to resist any attempt to deprive anyone of that for which we all long—freedom, equality and peace—and reduce our efforts to nothing. It was the policies of segregation that deprived those with disabilities of freedom, equality and peace, and the residential institutions and special hospitals were a manifestation of these policies. Deinstitutionalization and community living was the aim and also the means for protecting the rights expressed in the eight basic points of the normalization principle, and represented the social practice necessary for exercising our universal human rights. Accordingly, normalization means deinstitutionalization and community living. Empowerment and independent living, which emerged from the 1980s, are a philosophy and a movement that were adopted to further accelerate this process. In that sense, we can see empowerment, independent living and the normalization principle as part of the same continuum.

Notes

1) Quoted from the Keno Fukushikai Association webpage of April 2007 (http://tomoni.or.jp/index.php). On Sept. 5, 2012, a further shift was evident in the ideals underpinning the actions of this social welfare foundation, as follows:
"Aiming for a society in which every person's life is affirmed.
From the realization of normalization to the creation of social inclusion."
2) Quoted from the Nagano Shogaisha Seikatsu Shien Kyokai Association website on Sept. 5, 2012. (http://www.moritoki.jp/subl.html)
3) This chapter is based on the following publications which were revised for this purpose.
Katoda, Hiroshi (2010). "Nomaraizeshon genri saiko" (The Normalization Principle 'Reconsidered'). *Rikkyo Social Welfare Review*, Vol. 29, pp. 5-13.
Katoda, Hiroshi (2009). "Nomaraizeshon genri no chichi ron" (The Father of the Normalization Principle), *Rikkyo University College of Community and Human Services Bulletin*, Vol. 11, pp. 15-28. Rikkyo University College of Community and Human Services.
4) Papers on the 1946 normalization principle are as follows:
Katoda, Hiroshi (2005). "Shinsetsu 1946 nomaraizeshon no genri" (The New Theory of the 1946 Normalization Principle). *Bulletin of the College of Community and Human Services, Rikkyo University* 7: 13-23.
Katoda, Hiroshi (2009). *Nomaraizeshon genre to wa nanika (What is the Normalization Principle?)*. Chapter 2 pp. 28-41. Gendai Shokan.
5) The papers from 1985, 1986, 1992, and 2002 by Ericsson are as follows:
Ericsson, Kent (1985a). *The origin and consequences of the normalization principle.* IASSMD Congress. New Delhi, India.
Ericsson, Kent (1985b). *The Principle of Normalization: History and Experiences in Scandinavian Countries.* ILSMH Congress. Hamburg, Germany.
The following Japanese translation exists for the 1985b paper:
Katoda, H., Iwai, N., Sato, M., Hojo, R. (translation) (2012). "Nomaraizeshon genri: hokuo shokoku ni okeru genritenkai to keiken kara no manabi". *Bulletin of the College of Community and Human Services, Rikkyo University* 14, pp. 141-154.
Ericsson, Kent (1986). Omsorger för förståndshandikappades samhällsdeltagande (Special services for the mentally retarded). *Socialmedicinsk tidskrift* 1-2 : 11-16.

Ericsson, Kent (1992). *Housing for the persons with intellectual handicap: Consequences of a citizen perspective*. Paper presented at the AAMR Annual Meeting, New Orleans.

Ericsson, Kent (2002). *From Institutional Life to Community Participation*. Acta Universitatis Upsaliensis, Uppsala Studies in Education 99.

The 2002 publication was Ericsson's doctorate thesis for which there is a Japanese translation as follows:

Katoda, H., Koseki-Dahl, M. (translation) (2012). *Sweden ni okeru shisetsu kaitai to chiiki seikatsu shien – shisetsu karusurundo no tanjo to kaitai made wo yoridokoroni* (Deinstitutionalization and Community Living in Sweden: Based on the Process the Led from the Establishment to the Dissolution of Carlslund). Gendai Shokan.

6) Statens Offentliga Utredningar (SOU) (1946:24). *Kommitténs för Partiellt Arbetsföra Betänkande I* (The committee for the partially able-bodied. Report I). Socialdepartmentet.

In response to the committee's report (SOU1946:24), the following reports were published, leading to the enactment and adoption of Lag om undervisning och vård av vissa psykiskt efterblivna (Act on education and care of some mentally subnormal, 1954:483) in 1954 and the 1955 report of the 1951 Committee on the care of the mentally subnormal (see note 11) and the establishment of a set of services.

SOU1947:18. *Kommitténs för Partiellt Arbetsföra Betänkande II* (The committee for the partially able-bodied. Report II).

SOU1947:44. *Kommitténs för Partiellt Arbetsföra Betänkande III* (The committee for the partially able-bodied. Report III).

SOU1949:11. *Betänkande om Sinneslövården avgivet av 1946 års sinneslövårdsutredning* (Report concerning care of the feebleminded prepared by the 1946 Enquiry on the care of the feebleminded).

Kommitténs för partiellt arbetsföra. (1949). *Partiellt arbetsföras problem: En översikt över kommitténs för partiellt arbetsföras förslag* (The problem of the partially able-bodied. A review of the proposal from the committee for the partially able-bodied).

Considering that the above reports are intimately related to the 1954 Act on education and care of some mentally subnormal, it is clear that the Committee on employment for the partially ablebodied, which was established in 1943, laid the foundation for the social services for the disabled in Sweden today.

7) cf. op. cit. (SOU1946:24), p. 12.
8) ibid, p. 28.

9) Kommitténs för partiellt arbetsföra (1949). *Partiellt arbetsföras problem: En översikt över kommitténs för partiellt arbetsföras förslag* (The problem of the partially able-bodied. A review of the proposal from the committee for the partially able-bodied).

10) ibid, p. 21.

11) The 1955 report of the 1951 Committee on the care of the feebleminded is as follows: 1951 års sinnesslövårdsutredning (1955). *Betänkande III med utredning och förslag rörande den öppna vården av psykiskt efterblivna samt utbildning av viss vårdpersonal* (Committee report III including enquiry and proposal regarding open care for the mentally subnormal and the training of certain care staff). Stockholm: Inrikesdepartementet.

A document appended to this report is attributed to Bergh. This is Albert Bergh, a member of the 1951 Committee on the care of the feebleminded. One of his papers was also appended to the 1946 report.

Bergh, A. (1946). Arbetsvården för beredskapsinvaliderna (Employment rehabilitation for the disabled). In: SOU1946:24. *Kommitténs för Partiellt Arbetsföra Betänkande I.* Socialdepartmentet, Bilaga 4, 184-198.

The appendix by Bergh attached to the 1955 report of the above committee is as follows: Bergh, Albert (1955). De olika arbetsvårdsformerna (The different forms of employment rehabilitation). In: 1951 års sinnesslövårdsutredning (1955). *Betänkande III med utredning och förslag rörande den öppna vården av psykiskt efterblivna samt utbildning av viss vårdpersonal* (Committee Report III including enquiry and recommendations regarding open care for the mentally subnormal and the training of certain care staff). Stockholm: Inrikesdepartementet, Bilaga 5, 1-9.

12) cf. ob. cit. (Ericsson, 2002), p. 41.

Ericsson quotes from the 1952 report by the 1951 Committee on the care of the mentally subnormal (p.15):

1951 års sinnesslövårdsutredning. 1952. *Betänkande med förslag till Lag om undervisning och vård av vissa psykiskt efterblivna m.m.* (Committee report with proposal on legislation regarding education and care of some mentally subnormal etc.). Stockholm: Inrikesdepartementet.

13) cf. ob. cit. (Ericsson, 2002), p.31.

14) ibid, p. 32.

15) The Act concerning the Care of the Mentally Retarded and other exceptionally Retarded Persons, 1959:192.

16) In the following document related to the above 1959 Act, there is the following statement: "...to create a situation for the handicapped as near to the normal as possible, irrespective of whether it occurs entirely or partly within the institution or out in the community." (Socialministeriet (1959). *CirkulÆre om forsorger for åndsvage og andre særlig svagtbegavede*. P.7. Köpenhamn: Socialministeriet. English from cf. ob. cit. (Ericsson, 2002), p.32.

17) SFS 1967:940. Lag om omsorger om visa psykiskt utvecklingsstörda (Act on Special Services for the Mentally Retarded).

18) Nirje, B. (1992). Introduction. In B. Nirje, *The Normalization Principle Papers*. Uppsala universitet. (From the Japanese translation by H. Katoda (1998). *Nomaraizeshon no genri*. Gendai Shokan. pp.5-21.

19) Nirje, B. (1969). The Normalization Principle and Its Human Management Implications. In R. B. Kugel & W. Wolfensberger (eds.). *Changing Patterns in Residential Services for the Mentally Retarded*. pp. 51-57. Washington D.C.: President's Committee on Mental Retardation. (From the new revised edition of the Japanese translation by H. Katoda (2004). *Nomaraizeshon genri – fuhenka to shakaihenkaku wo motomete*. Gendai Shokan. Chapter 1, pp.22-32.)

20) Wolfensberger, W. (1972). *Normalization: The Principle of Normalization in Human Services*. Toronto: National Institute on Mental Retardation. (From the Japanese translation by Y. Nakasono, S. Shimizu (1982). *Nomaraizeshon*. Gakuensha. p. 48.)

21) ibid, p. 49.

22) Kugel, R.B. & Wolfensberger, W. (eds.). 1969. *Changing Patterns in Residential Services for the Mentally Retarded*. Washington D.C.: President's Committee on Mental Retardation.

23) Dybwad, G.. (1969). Action implications, U.S.A. today. In R. B. Kugel & W. Wolfensberger (eds.). *Changing Patterns in Residential Services for the Mentally Retarded*. Washington D.C.: President's Committee on Mental Retardation. Full Text page 1-13.

24) ibid (Dybwad. DHM: Library). Full Text page 1 no. 5.

25) cf. ob. cit. (Nirje 1969), p.181. (H. Katoda, trans. (2004), pp.22-23.)

26) ibid, pp. 23-28.

27) Nirje, B. (1985). The basis and logic of the normalization principle. *Australia and New Zealand Journa of Developmental Disabilities*, vol 11, no.2, pp.65-68. (p.67)

28) ibid, p. 130.

29) ibid, p. 125.

30) ibid, p. 130.
31) ibid, p. 127.
32) ibid, p. 132.
33) Bank-Mikkelsen, N. E. (1969). A metropolitan area in Denmark. In Kugel, R.B. & Wolfensberger, W. (eds.), *Changing Patterns in Residential Services for the Mentally Retarded*. Washington D.C.: President's Committee on Mental Retardation. (DHM:Library, Collection: Documents – Full Text page 1 no.10)
34) Bank-Mikkelsen, N. E. (1976). The Principle of Normalization. In Nielsen, B. (ed.), *Flash on the Danish National Service for the Mentally Retarded II*. No.39. Copenhagen: Personal Training School. (Y. Nakazono translation. (1978). "Nomaraizeshon no genri". *Shikoku Gakuin University Treatises*, Vol. 42. pp.43-153, p. 146. 1978.)
35) ibid, p. 153.
36) Nirje, B. (2003). *Normaliseringsprincipen* (The normalization principle). Lund: Studentlitteratur AB.
37) Söder, M.. 2003. Kap 9: Normalisering, handikappolitik och forskning (Chapter 9: Normalization, Disability Policy and Research). In B. Nirje, *Normaliseringsprincipen*. P. 191. Lund: Studentlitteratur AB. (Y. Hanson translation. (2008). *Saiko/nomaraizeshon no genri – sono hirogari to gendaiteki igi* (Normalization Principle: Its Spread and Contemporary Significance). Gendai Shokan. P. 24, 2008.
Kristiansen is quoted from the following:
Kristiansen, K. (1994). *Normalisering og Verdesetjing av Social Rolle* (Normalization and Social Role Valorization). Oslo: Kommuneforlaget.
38) ibid, p. 191 (p. 222, 2008 translation)
39) ibid, (p. 223, 2008 translation)
40) ibid, pp. 191-192.
41) ibid, p.192 (quoted from SOU:1980:34 p. 79)
42) ibid, (quoted from Beredningsgruppen för internationella handikappåret 1981, p. 9) (p. 224, 2008 translation)
43) ibid.
44) ibid, p.193.
45) ibid, (p. 225, 2008 translation)
46) ibid.
47) ibid, pp. 194-195 (pp. 225-227, 2008 translation)

For this section, I quoted or summarized the Japanese translation on pages 24 and 25 and revised those portions where the meaning was unclear by comparing them to the original text.
48) Ratzka, A. D. (1986). *Independent Living and Attendant Care in Sweden: A Consumer Perspective.* New York: World Rehabilitation Fund. (H. Katoda, M. Koseki-Dahl translation. (1991). *Sueden ni okeru jiritsu seikatsu to pasonaru/ashisutansu – tojisha kanri no ronri.* Gendai Shokan.)
49) ibid, p. 87.
50) ibid, pp. 88. 1991 translation.
51) cf. ob. cit. (Söder. 2003), p. 207.
Oliver is quoted from the following:
Oliver, M. (1999). Capitalism, disability and ideology: A materialist critique of the Normalization principle. In R. J. Flynn & R. A. Lemay (eds.). *A Quarter-Century of Normalization and Social Role Valorization; Evolution and Impact.* Ottawa: University of Ottawa Press.

Chapter 2
Deinstitutionalization and Community Living in Sweden

Section 1 Legislation of the Normalization Principle and Deinstitutionalization and Community Living

1. Changes in the Swedish Legal System and Deinstitutionalization and Community Living Policies

Despite its reputation as a welfare state, until the late 1960s the social environment in Sweden for people with intellectual disabilities was far from satisfactory.[1] This was the era when residential institutions were at their peak. Community welfare services were inadequate, education for all was not yet compulsory, and opportunities for employment and leisure were deplorably lacking. Having a intellectual disability meant being relegated to the margins of society and deprived of the various rights required to live as an equal member of society. For example, in the 1944 Act on Education and Care of the Educable Feebleminded[2] (hereunder the 1944 Act), education was to be provided only for "feebleminded" children who were considered "educable", while the "uneducable" were to be provided with private "occupational homes" and "asylums" (both of which were equivalent to current residential institutions).[3] The term "educable" fell out of use with the 1954 Act on Education and Care of Some Mentally Subnormal[4] (hereunder the "1954 Act"), and compulsory education provided by the state was extended to people with moderate intellectual disabilities.[5] Under the 1954 Act, residential institutions were governed by the public system, a move that actually resulted in an increase in the scale of residential homes.

The normalization principle was the focus of debate among public committees in Sweden from the mid-1940s to the mid-1950s. In the 1960s, this debate recurred, but this time it was focused predominantly on demanding new and better quality legislation. The result was the Act on Special Services for Some Mentally Retarded[6] (hereunder the

"Special Services Act"), which was enacted in 1967. This was the first Act in Sweden to incorporate the content of the normalization principle. Its historical significance lay in its establishment of an education system for all school-age children, its measures for improving the quality of the living environment (by reviewing the institution-centered approach to care and introducing alternatives in the form of group homes, the small group system, and personal care programs), and its introduction of a new concept in social services for the intellectually impaired that represented a shift from "care" to "support". The fact that Nirje included the entire Special Services Act as an appendix to the English translation of his thesis on the normalization principle[7] indicates that he considered it an example of the principle's concrete realization.

After implementation of the Special Services Act (1968), education for people with intellectual disabilities gradually shifted from special schools to integration within ordinary schools, while services shifted from care provided in residential institutions to group homes within the community. This shift brought to the fore several issues[8], including 1) the inferior legal status of group homes compared with residential institutions, 2) lack of coherency in services due to the dispersion of service responsibility among the state, county and municipality, and 3) inadequate human rights protection due to the designation of the law and the services contained therein as "special". In response to these issues, the government established the Committee on Special Services[9] in 1977 to consider the nature and types of concrete supports required based on the normalization concept.

The discussions of the 1977 Committee influenced the content of the 1980 Act on Social Services (enacted in 1982, revised in 2001), a point that is clearly evident when examining the Proposition on the Act on Social Services[10] submitted to parliament in 1979 (prop 1979/80:1). The draft states:

> "A good residence is a prerequisite for people with disabilities to participate in the life of the community and tolive like other people. The objective of housing policies should be that all people have their own dwelling. Residential institutions in which people with disabilities live together are clearly behind the times. These

inherent distinctiveness is contrary to fundamental values. The long years of effort to eradicate residential institutions must continue into the future."[11]

The deliberations of the Committee on Special Services resulted in the Act on Special Services for the Mentally Retarded and Others (hereunder the "New Special Services Act")[12], which was enacted in 1985.

There are several features of the New Special Services Act that are worthy of mention. These are: the extension of services beyond the mentally retarded to those with acquired intellectual impairments and children with mental illnesses (children with autism probably fell into this category); the delineation of special rights and their content; the recognition of the right of the person receiving services to self-determination, the right to appeal (if dissatisfied with the content of supports) and concrete measures for the realization of various rights; clarification of the shift in social services from institution-based to community-based care and of the policy for dissolving and closing residential institutions; identification of concrete measures for providing both the material supports and support staff necessary for community living; and, the direction for an administrative decentralization of provisions of various measures. It is clear from the content that the normalization principle has been incorporated as visible, concrete legislative measures. This New Act also resolved issues 1) and 2) above, which were inherent to the Special Services Act. As for problem 3), while the New Act determined that special services did not constitute discrimination against the receiver[13], it lacked concrete guarantees for special services and punitive clauses concerning failure to provide such services. Still, the New Special Services Act strove to improve every facet of the daily lives of people with intellectual disabilities, including housing, education, employment and leisure, so that with the support of special services the intellectually disabled could enjoy, as far as possible, a lifestyle with the same rhythm, environment and economic standard as that of the general public.

In 1989, the Committee on Handicaps[14] was established to explore new forward-looking measures for people with disabilities based on previous developments concerning the normalization principle. The Committee published a number of reports, which were compiled in the 1991 report *Handicap, Welfare, and Justice*[15] and the final report of 1992, *One Society for All*[16]. These two reports formed the core of the "Act Concerning Support and Service for Persons with Certain Functional Impairments"[17] (hereunder LSS) enacted in 1993.

The LSS, which came into effect on January 1, 1994, replaced the New Special Services Act and contains many features that are not found in the latter. The first of these is the introduction of a new concept concerning the content of services and supports that moves away from "support" to "fulfillment of rights" and further clarifies the subject and content of "the right to self-determination". The second new feature was the use of the expression "functional impairment" and the wider range of people encompassed by the legislation. Specifically, the LSS was extended to cover all people with disabilities, including children and adults with severe physical disabilities and with severe mental and physical disorders in addition to those included under the New Special Services Act. The third new feature was the directive obliging all counties to submit a plan by December 31, 1994 for dissolving special hospitals and residential institutions. This directive strengthened the policy of dissolving and closing residential institutions laid out in the New Special Services Act. The fourth new feature was charging partial fees for welfare services (this also applied to part of the services provided under the Act on Social Services). Considering that people who required special support were not charged for services from the Special Services Act up to the New Special Services Act, this represented a major change in Sweden's social welfare services. The fifth feature was the introduction of a personal assistance system which demonstrates that the government was exploring how to provide consumer-controlled supports and services. This type of approach was being experimented with in the field of services for people with physical disabilities, and attempts at consumer control were drawing increasing attention and gradually being expanded. But with the introduction of this system under the LSS, the movement was extended to disabilities of all types, and the impact on supports and services can only be called revolutionary. Further, the Assistance Benefit Act[18] (hereunder LASS) was enacted with the introduction of this system. One other feature worthy of mention is the Disability Ombudsman Act.[19] This Act, which came into force on July 1, 1994, provided access to public transport and prohibited discrimination against people with disabilities. (Under the Discrimination Act[20] enforced from January 1, 2009, this was renamed Equality Ombudsman[21]) Through the realization of these systems, the fulfillment of the rights of people with functional impairments became ever closer to reality.

The draft Act on Social Services, which defined the perspective that led to the dissolution of residential institutions, the New Special Services Act, which defined the policy for dissolution and closure, and the LSS, which ordered special hospitals and residential institutions to submit (by December 31, 1994) a concrete plan for the same, led to the enactment and enforcement of the Act on Closure of Special Subnormality Hospitals and Residential Homes[22] in 1997, and by the end of December 1999, the dismantling of special hospitals and residential institutions was decided. Measures for post-institution community based living were provided by the Act on Social Services (enacted in 1980, enforced from 1982 and revised in 2001), the LSS and LASS.

2. Why Residential Institutions Were Dissolved

Clearly, the principle of normalization exerted a major influence in the dissolving of residential institutions and the establishment of community living support measures from the drafting of the Act on Social Services right through to the enactment of the LSS, LASS, and the Act on Closure of Special Subnormality Hospitals and Residential Homes. By nature, every human being, regardless of whether they have a disability or not, has the right to the same conditions of daily life as the general public, including the right to have their own residence, to be ensured a place of work (or daily activity), and to enjoy leisure activities. No one should be relegated by others to live in a special environment. In fact, however, residential institutions represent a special environment, one in which all the spaces and conditions of daily life from one's residence and work to interactions with others and leisure activities are contained within the same space. Sweden's Ministry of Health and Social Affairs summed up the reasons for dissolving the institutions through a comparison of institution-based supports versus community-based supports[23] as follows:

(1) Making the invisible visible

In residential institutions, residents are often lumped together as a large group because conditions make it difficult to distinguish or understand them as individuals.

In the community, people with disabilities live in small group homes and are respected as individuals. They are more emotionally stable, and any problems they experience can be recognized readily and necessary improvements made. People with intellectual disabilities and staff members are all members of society, and as such they are viewed with more interest by the people in their community.

(2) From isolation to being a member of society

Most residential institutions are segregated and distant from the local community (even if they are located in the center of town). As a result, they tend to develop their own distinct culture with its own rules and management system over which it is difficult for society to exert control.

In the community, it is easier to communicate and to participate in society. Contact with others is a natural part of daily life. As individuals gain access to various types of assistance and cooperation, conditions for using social resources increase.

(3) From mechanical to varied work

In residential institutions, there is too little room for variation, which often leads to ritualization of care work and few opportunities for spontaneous activities. As a result, people fall under the illusion that routine work fulfills the individual needs of the users.

In supported activities in the community, it becomes necessary to provide activities that place importance on the needs and interests of the individual rather than on routine tasks.

(4) From intensive management to management dispersed in the community

In residential institutions, the system of instruction is geared to the group and the environment is closed and complete within itself. Most residential institutions develop a bureaucratic structure in which the living wards do not have autonomy and in which activities are dominated by the wishes of those in authority.

With supported activities in the community, daily activities and recreation are carried out in a variety of spaces and living environments, and staff members have a variety of roles. In the community, the staff members interact with staffgroups outside care situations and face new expectations.

(5) From care to social support services

Residential institutions are influenced by a medical-centered approach, and experts usually decide the content of activities. These are generally stipulated by physical rather than social factors, and the tendency is for rationalization to be given priority in care.

In the community, the individual must decide the form and content of supports, and therefore qualitative changes occur in the role of staff members. Experts work as consultant or supervisor. Staff members also gain confidence, develop social relations, enjoy the variation in their work and experience greater satisfaction. In addition, their work comes to be valued by society.

(6) From inequality to respect of the individual's wishes

In the residential institution, the residential wards are basically a place of work for the staff members, which results in more control and restrictions on the users' needs. Users have almost no personal belongings. Most things are used communally, and users do not even have the right to own their own bed.

In the community, there are increased opportunities and conditions for respecting the wishes and interests of people with intellectual disabilities. The individual can have his or her own residence, and users are provided with better quality and higher material standards, a better economic level per person, and a larger living space. It is easier for the users to convey their wishes regarding their own residence and to participate in the activities of daily life. Staff members are able to more accurately grasp the needs and wishes of each individual.

These six reasons for dissolving residential institutions also represented a perfect summary of the structural characteristics of institutions and brought the very meaning of their existence into question. They also indicated that reforms could never eliminate this structural framework and that therefore the approach must shift towards the dissolution of residential institutions.

3. Towards Measures for Inclusion in the Community through Collaborative Measures

Developments in social services for the intellectually disabled in Sweden from the 1944 Act to the present day can be summarized in the points outlined below.

The first point is the shift away from discrimination towards equality. This shift also represented the basic philosophy that laid the framework for the normalization principle and brought it into being. The second point is the movement away from institutions and towards the community. Within this movement, Sweden chose the bold path of dismantling and closing special hospitals and residential institutions and establishing a system of diverse services for support in the home. The third point was a major change from welfare services proposed by representatives of the users to those proposed by the users themselves. The fourth point was the clear delineation of the rights of the receiver of the services as the focus moved away from care to support and further to fulfillment of the individual's rights. The concepts of user participation and self-determination, which were defined through trying to fulfill those rights, can be viewed as the culmination of the normalization principle. The fifth point was the decentralization of the provision of social services and supports, which was delegated to the local level. Decentralization was intended to provide rational and integrated services, and it did indicate one route towards the realization of thorough social services and integration.

These features and their ultimate destination represent the result of many years of effort by the Swedish people involved in this field beginning from the 1940s as they explored such questions as the meaning of normalization, the necessary legislative measures to make it a reality, and the measures required for deinstitutionalization and community living.

In the Act on Closure of Special Subnormality Hospitals and Residential Homes established in 1997, it was clearly stated that "all residential institutions will be dissolved by December 31, 1999." In documents published by Sweden's bureau of statistics in 2000, there is no mention of residential institutions to be found. At least at a statistical level, residential institutions had ceased to exist. Residents of group homes located on the grounds of former institutions, which were not counted in the statistics, were gradually relocated to group homes in the cities, and former residents of institutions were in the real sense of the term beginning to live in the community. Naturally, of course, the movement to dismantle the institutions caused changes not only in the place of residence but also in the place of daily activity, the nature of leisure and cultural activities, and the nature of human relationships due to the strengthening and consolidation of individual plans-to further improve quality of life.

However, in order for people with disabilities to be assured of an ordinary life in the community and the fulfillment of their various rights, ceaseless efforts to establish interaction between the disabled and those around them (including society) and to improve their living environment are essential. These efforts naturally include the establishment of physical supports, human resources and social support systems for post-deinstitutionalization community living. This alone, however, is not enough to solve various social problems or to change people's hearts or their relationships with others. It is only through "collaborative" measures that "understanding" and "caring" are born and 1) dignity, 2) social acceptance, 3) recognition of needs, 4) social roles and expectations, 5) social valuation and satisfaction, and 6) respect for the wishes of each individual are nurtured, leading to "inclusion".

Section 2 The Dissolution of Carlslund and Deinstitutionalization Policies in Sweden

The purpose of this section is to clarify the role of the residential institution called Carlslund, which was located in northwest Stockholm, Sweden, the effect that its dissolution had on Sweden's social welfare policies for the disabled, the reason Sweden succeeded in dismantling Carlslund in the first place, and the process by which it did so while developing, from the 1940s onward, the legislation that would give shape to the normalization principle and establish the measures required for deinstitutionalization and community living. For this purpose, I will: (1) present an overview of historical developments in the move towards deinstitutionalization in Sweden as seen through official documents; (2) present an overview of the process of the dissolution of Carlslund, which represents a model case for deinstitutionalization in Sweden; and, (3) examine the conditions required for dismantling residential institutions gleaned from the dissolution of Carlslund.[24]

1. The Dissolution of Residential Institutions in Sweden as Seen through Official Documents

One official document that referred to the normalization principle and offered a proposal that led to the dismantling of residential institutions can be found in materials published in 1958 by the Stockholm county headquarters for the education, care and support of the mentally retarded. The document was written by Hjalmar Mehr and it states:

> A happy community ... As in the community at large, life consists of leisure and work. Children go to their "school", adults to their "work" ...They have the same right as all others to live a secure and full life ... It is the duty of society to provide resources so that the life for each one can be as favorable as possible."[25]

The content of Mehr's proposal is in essence the normalization principle. It appears, however, to have been ahead of its time, and it would take almost a full decade before it would be accepted by Stockholm County and by those involved in the field throughout Sweden. In 1968, the Act on Special Services for the Mentally Retarded (hereunder the Special Services Act) came into effect and efforts to move from residential institutions to the community accelerated rapidly. Under this law, integration was pushed forward, and everyone, regardless of whether they had a disability or not, was able to attend school. (cf. Under the 1944 Act, prior to the Special Services Act, only people with mild disabilities were assured the right to an education, while the 1954 Act extended this right to people with moderate disabilities.) In addition, many group homes were built.

In the 1970s, the nature of the residential institution was seriously debated, and the shift from improving such institutions towards their dissolution gradually became more pronounced. Around this time, official documents referring to the dissolution of residential institutions can be found at the national level. In the 1979 draft of the Act on Social Services, which I mentioned in the first section, we find the expression "long years of effort towards eliminating residential institutions", which indicates this shift towards dissolution. This content was incorporated in the Act on Social Services established in 1980 (enforced in 1982), and although the term "residential institution" was not used, the concept that the realization of the normalization principle=the closure and dissolution of residential institutions=relocation to and living in the community is incorporated in every article of that legislation.

> Official public services must be established as the foundation of democracy and solidarity and promote individuals' economic and social security, equality of living conditions and active participation in local society. Moreover, social services should be based on self-determination of the individual and respect for integrity.[26]

> People with physical or mental disabilities should participate in the life of the local community and should be given the opportunity to lead a normal life as far as possible.[27]

Further, a handbook on issues concerning people with disabilities, which was published by the Ministry of Health and Social Affairs in 1982, states that:

> Society must develop in such a way that inequality is eradicated and people have equal living conditions so that all people can contribute to development and be involved in the community in some form... In order for general policy

objectives to be made applicable to people with functional impairments, measures established by policies for the disabled must be applicable to diverse social fields and in harmony with other policies."[28]

The vision of dissolution of residential institutions as the culmination of the practical application of the normalization principle was also applied to the field of intellectual disabilities, and the dissolution of residential facilities and special hospitals was explicitly stipulated for the first time in the 1985 New Special Services Act as well as the Introductory Act for enforcing it.

> Residential institutions for children and youth will be closed without delay. Nor will they accept new residents. Residential institutions and special hospitals for adults will be closed when economic conditions and concerns for their residents permit. New residents will only be accepted under special circumstances. Family homes will be for children only.[29]

In 1989, the Committee on Special Services was established to revise the New Special Services Act.[30] The committee's report presented the following proposal concerning the dissolution of residential institutions and special hospitals.

> The dissolution of residential institutions in many counties is still being examined... The deadline for ensuring a form of residence to replace the residential institution is January 1, 1998. Plans for dissolving residential institutions must be submitted by December 31, 1993 at the latest.[31]

The outcome of the final report[32] from the Committee on Special Services was the Act Concerning Support and Service for Persons with Certain Functional Impairments (hereunder LSS[33]) which was adopted in May 1993 (and implemented in 1994) and the LSS Introductory Act.[34] Regarding the dissolution of residential institutions, the latter Act states:

The county and city must cooperate and plan for the dissolution of existing special hospitals and residential institutions. The dissolution plan must be prepared and submitted to the Ministry of Health and Social Affairs by December 31, 1994.[35]

Through the implementation of the LSS, the right to supports and services was clarified, and the content of that right was more concretely defined. The style of residence changed. In group homes, each individual was not only entitled to their own room but was also given a functional living space much like that of a single dwelling. The LSS introduced the personal assistance system, which provided a personal assistant twenty-four-hours a day where needed. This system allowed people with severe functional disabilities to use a personal assistant as much as necessary with funding by the municipal and national governments.

In 1997, the Act on Closure of Special Subnormality Hospitals and Residential Homes was adopted and implemented and the move towards dissolution became inevitable due to the inclusion of the following clause: "All residential institutions will be dissolved by December 31, 1999." As a result, the number of residents in institutions dropped drastically from 19,000 in 1964 to 8,000 in 1985 (a 40 percent reduction) and to one-tenth or 1,785 residents in 1995. On January 1, 2000, only 86 people remained in group homes located on the grounds of former institutions. Almost all of these have since been relocated to the group homes in the community.

The dissolution of residential institutions took a step towards realization with the New Special Services Act in 1986, and was ensured by two subsequent laws with legal force (the 1994 LLS and the 1997 Act on Closure of Special Subnormality Hospitals and Residential Homes). It was Carlslund, an institution located in northern Stockholm County that imparted the breath of dissolution into the New Special Services Act and became a model case for dissolving residential institutions. From the 1970s, Carlslund reduced the number of residents. It established The Project for the Closure of the Institution to pursue closure and dissolution and, from 1981, proceeded systematically towards this goal. The next section reviews the process[36] from the birth of Carlslund to its dissolution.

2. The Dissolution of Carlslund, a Model Case

Carlslund was established in 1901 by Maria Krantzon. At the time, it consisted of only 8 users and 4 nursing staff. Through the efforts of its founder, however, the content was gradually enhanced. After the death of Mrs. Krantzon in 1925, the city of Stockholm (later Stockholm County) gradually became involved in the institution's operation. As a result, the scale of the facility increased, expanding to 42 residents in 1931 and to 172 by the end of the 1940s. This trend was related to the implementation of the Act on Education and Care of Some Mentally Subnormal 1954 and the conversion of residential homes into public institutions. By 1964, it accommodated 524 people with intellectual disabilities. At the same time, and despite the trend towards enlarging such institutions, Carlslund had begun experimenting with group homes within the grounds. Yet, although the scale of residence was smaller, regardless of the size, the lives of those who lived there were still a far cry from the lifestyle of the general public. Visitors came from America, the Soviet Union and Japan, with the intention of using Carlslund as a model for colony style construction.[37] Ironically, Sweden was to undertake a major reform of residential institutions a few years later, changing course towards the dissolution of such homes. Those involved in social services in Japan and other countries, however, had no way of knowing this.

After implementation of the Special Services Act in 1968, which was based on the normalization principle, the number of users decreased annually. Group homes within residential institutions had already taken root under the previous Act, and residents and staff began to relocate gradually to small-scale communal homes (community group homes) in town.[38] Carlslund became the first residential institution to achieve dissolution, and, as such, it also came to be seen as a model case for relocation to the community. It is clear that Carlslund not only experimented with group homes within the institution, but also implemented a wide range of social training programs at its daytime activity center and encouraged self-government activities by the users in the belief that these were important to the socialization process.

The group homes within the institution were organized for one, two, three, four and five persons, depending on the users' degree of independence and disability, and even in the terrace house style of wards, which housed 15 to 20 users, the users were reorganized into 5-people units. When I visited in 1983, the fruits of deinstitutionalization were already evident with the number of residents having dropped to less than half (from 524 to 250). Kent Ericsson, who wrote the blueprints for Carlslund's dissolution and who served as the leader of the closure project, told me during our discussions that the group homes within the institution were just one step in the dissolution process and that not all institutions necessarily needed to take the same route to achieve dissolution.

The downsizing of residential institutions and relocation to the community, which started in the early 1970s, evolved to the point where a special committee was established in Stockholm County to consider improvements for the care of people with intellectual disabilities. In 1976, the committee published a report and it was decided that Carlslund would be closed and dissolved. At the time, the number of residents had already decreased to 350.[39] In 1978, by which time there were only 322 residents, the project team for dissolution announced a plan for the relocation of the remaining residents to the community based on the county's policy.[40] The blueprint of the project team was to gradually return the remaining residents, projected at 301 by 1981, to the community and to complete dissolution by 1988. While deinstitutionalization did not proceed exactly as planned, its realization was achieved through consultations among the plan's proposers, representatives of the institution's staff, user representatives, and management.

In 1985, half of Carlslund's grounds were sold for regular housing and transformed into Carlslund Town. Finally, on March 11, 1988, Carlslund residential home ceased to exist. That day I happened to phone the Carlslund Center for people with Disabilities in order to make an appointment to visit. The person who took my call said, "I'm sorry but the residential home no longer exists. Today, two people will transfer to a group home in the community and once they are gone, the institution will vanish forever." From April 22 to 24, 1988, a public talk and exhibition was held on the site to commemorate the dissolution of Carlslund. Attending this event gave me an overall picture of the process of its dissolution.

The extensive grounds of the Carlslund residential home were situated on a small wooded hill. The existing buildings were renovated, and trees were cut down to make way for new buildings. Buildings on the other side of the hill were left as is, and were used as the northwest sector support office with a cafeteria and staff training building. Because the new Carlslund Town was separated by a hill from the grounds where the old buildings and facilities remained, visitors to the area rarely see the latter and might be misled into believing that the entire institution was transformed into a residential district. The structure has not changed much since that time.

Carlslund Town was envisioned as a model of an integrated residential district with a diverse population of people of all ages that included the physically or intellectually disabled. It was also designed so that people with intellectual disabilities would comprise less than one percent of the population within a single residential area. (There are 320 households living in Carlslund Town.)

Seventeen people remain in the Carlslund facility within Carlslund Town. The others have all relocated to community group homes in Stockholm County. The project's concept was to return users to the area in which their parents lived or in which the user had lived for many years. This, however, was difficult to realize, and many former residents were relocated to newly built community group homes in consideration of the advanced age of their parents, the difficulty of acquiring land, and the sentiments of people in the community.

Of the seventeen remaining in Carlslund Town, five lived in a community group home for 5 people (1 location, 6 staff), 8 lived in 4 different 2-person community apartments (4 staff), and 4 lived in single-person community apartments (receiving assistance when necessary from staff members assigned to 5-person and 2-person dwellings). Every type of community group home available in Stockholm[41] at that time (types 07, 06, 05) was established in Carlslund Town. Type 05 was a semi-independent living style arrangement in which users could receive assistance as needed. Type 05 group homes generally housed about 8 people (with private individual rooms) with support provided by 1 to 2 staff members, who either lived in the same building or were posted to a nearby office. Type 06 generally housed about 8 people (with private rooms) and had 3 or 4 staff members to provide assistance primarily in the morning and evenings. Type 07 was for people who needed 24-hour assistance, and ordinarily 5 residents (with private rooms) were supported by 6 staff members to live in town. Type 07 group homes were for people with quite severe disabilities, and depending on the degree of disability, up to 13 staff members might be assigned to provide support. Of the original residents of Carlslund residential home who were relocated to community based group homes in Carlslund Town, only a handful remain. Most have passed away due to advanced age. In their stead, graduates of special schools and people with intellectual disabilities from other areas are now living here. The nature of the group home has changed significantly. The types listed above no longer exist. Now, many people with intellectual disabilities (76% in 2007) live in community group homes with large specialized functional spaces (35 to 47 m^2 rooms with an entranceway, kitchen, bedroom, living room, bath and toilet).

Many of those who moved to community group homes commute to social enterprises in their area (SAMHALL: a state-owned Swedish company equivalent to welfare workshops in Japan) and day centers, where they can work or receive training, join various adult education courses, and enjoy educational and recreational activities. Many staff members who have observed the intellectually disabled users who now live in the community group homes note that: "There were some people who found it difficult to adjust to the community group home because of the sudden change in environment, but in the majority of cases, the transition went very well. It was a very good thing that they moved out of the restricted environment of the institution and into the community group home in town."[42]

Carlslund was not only the first example in Sweden of the dissolution of a large scale institution but also in the world. It received extensive media coverage and had a powerful impact on many other countries, which also began to phase out residential institutions. The Carlslund residential home is truly a model case for examining social service policies for people with disabilities.

3. Conditions for the Dissolution of Residential Institutions as Learned from Dissolution of Carlslund

Carlslund residential home, which began with just 8 users and 4 staff in 1901, subsequently became a publicly funded institution. In 1946, it was proposed that the institution be transformed into a colony, a shift which proceeded at a steady pace. By 1964, it had become a gigantic residential home for 522 people. When large scale institutions came under criticism, Carlslund was no exception. Accepting the criticisms, Carlslund began instituting such measures as creating group homes on the premises and relocating to the community until the institution was finally closed. During the process of dissolving the institution, the conditions that would make its dissolution possible also emerged. Here let us examine these conditions glimpsed through the process of Carlslund's dissolution while summarizing the content of a paper published by Ericsson in 2002.[43]

Residential institutions came under criticism from the late 1960s to the 1970s. From the 1970s to the 1980s, the nature of residential institutions was widely debated, and many articles critical of the institutions appeared in the mass media. These articles exposed the desperate conditions and the neglect residents were forced to endure due to lack of staff, government policies that did more harm than good, and the unacceptable excuses as well as the mental anguish on the part of those working for the institutions. These reports provided further fuel to the debate on how residential institutions should be. Investigations were conducted, and the efficacy of community based services and their application to people with severe disabilities, as well as the need for group homes and participation in daily activities, were pointed out.

After the government investigation in 1971, Stockholm County established a working group in 1975 to draft a plan for the future of Carlslund, which would improve the residential home and promote deinstitutionalization.[44] The committee's members consisted of representatives from the institution's management and staff, the county, and three politicians. The committee's goal was to completely renovate the institution to create a home for people with severe and extremely severe developmental disabilities, and plans were made to build a modern facility that would house 200 people. However, the opinion that the institution should be closed, that all residents should be relocated and made eligible to receive community based services, gradually gained strength. The idea's proponents claimed that as long as the conditions required for daily living were met everyone could live a normal life in the community while using social services. In the end, the committee decided to close Carlslund and relocate its residents to the community on three conditions: (1) that there was sufficient funding, (2) that sufficient community based services would be provided, and (3) that the necessary staff could be employed. Members of the project team for the dissolution of Carlslund were appointed and began tackling the various issues involved.

The issue of what services would be provided in place of the institution was critical. The closure and dissolution of the institution would only be made possible by the provision of appropriate services to people who had relocated. Accordingly, the project team's first job was to undertake a survey to identify the needs for services of each individual user. This was followed by a survey of institution staff to determine whether they would be interested in and able to continue working in the field after leaving the institution by providing services to support the users to live and work in the community. Based on this series of surveys, a report[45] was prepared, leading to the conclusion that it was possible to phase out Carlslund residential home.

It is difficult to pinpoint when measures for closure and dissolution began. The original plan was to expand the number of residents to 600, but fortunately this plan was never realized. After the number peaked at 522 in 1965, residents were gradually relocated to other institutions, and efforts were continued to further reduce group size. After deciding to phase out the institution in 1976, the number of residents steadily declined. The plan for dissolution announced in 1981 clearly stated that dissolution was possible if the legislations and the system needed for community based living were prepared, and if funding and support services were secured (including the provision of various types of small-scale group homes and daily activity centers, the improvement of recreation services, etc.).

Notes

1) The following manuscript was corrected and revised for section 1-1.
Katoda, Hiroshi. (1998). "Biographical Essay: The Formation and Development of the Normalization Principle and its Legislation in Sweden." pp. 164-192. In Nirje, Bengt (Katoda, Hiroshi. Translation). *Nomaraizeshon no genri (The Normalization Principle)*. Gendai Shokan.

2) SFS 1944:477 Lag om undervisning och vård av bildbara sinnesslöa. (Act on education and care of the educable feebleminded)

3) Kase, Susumu (1988). "Sweden ni okeru nomaraizeshon ni kansuru kenkyu I: 1967 nen engoho no ichizuke to shoki rinen" (Research I on Normalization in Sweden: The Role of the 1967 Special Services Act and Early Philosophy". 26th Japanese Association of Special Education Meeting.

4) SFS 1954:483 Lag om undervisning och vård av vissa psykiskt efterblivna. (Act on education and care of some mentally subnormal)

5) cf. op. cit. (Kase, 1988)

6) SFS 1967:940 Lag angående omsorger om vissa psykiskt utvecklingsstörda. (Act on special services for some mentally retarded)

7) Nirje, B (1969). "The Normalization Principle and its Human Management Implications". In R. B. Kugel and W. Wolfensberger. *Changing patterns in residential services for the mentally retarded*. Washington, D.C. President's Committee on Mental Retardation.

8) Kase, Susumu. Oi, Seikichi (1986). "Suweden ni okeru nomaraizeshon ni kansuru kenkyu II: 1967 nen seishin hattatsu chitaisha engoho kaisei wo tegakari toshite" (Research II on Normalization in Sweden: Using Clues from the 1967 Revised Special Services Act for the Mentally Retarded). 24th Japanese Association of Special Education Meeting.

9) Omsorgskommittén (The committee on special services). This committee prepared the following report, which offers glimpses of the content of the New Special Services Act: Omsorger om vissa handikappade. SOU 1981:26. *Betänkande från omsorgskommittén* (Report from the committee on special services).

10) The source for information concerning *Preposition om socialtjänstlag* (Proposition on the act on social services). (prop 1979/80:1) is from the following document:
Socialstyrelsen (1990:11). *Institutionsavveckling – Utvecklingsstörda personers flyttning från vårdhem* (Closure of the institution – Deinstitutionalization and community living for the mentally retarded).

11) ibid, p. 9.

12) SFS 1985:568 Lag om särskilda omsorger om psykiskt utvecklingsstörda m fl (Act on special services for the mentally retarded and others).
13) Cf. op. cit. (Kase. Oi. 1986)
14) Handikappkommitten (Committee on handicap).
15) Handikapputredning (1991). *Handikapp Välfärd Rättvisa* (Handicap, Welfare, Justice). (SOU 1991:46)
16) Handikapputredning (1992). *Ett samhälle för alla* (Society for all). (SOU 1992:52)
17) SFS 1993:387 Lag om stöd och service till vissa funktionshindrade (Act on cerning support and service for persons with certain functional impaiments).
18) SFS 1993:389 Lag om assistansersätning (Assistance Benefit Act).
19) SFS 1994:749 Lag om handikappombudsmannen (Act on Disability Ombudsman).
20) SFS 2008:567 Diskrimineringslag (Discrimination Act).
21) Diskrimineringsombudsmannen (Equality Ombudsman).
22) SFS 1997:724 Lag om avveckling av specialsjukhus och vårdhem (Act on closure of special subnormality hospitals and residential homes).
23) Cf. op. cit. (Socialstyrelsen, 1990). From the following abridged Japanese translation: H. Katoda (1994). "Sueden ni okeru nyusho shisetsu kaitai to chiiki seikatsu" (Dissolution of Residential Institutions in Sweden and Community Based Living). *Hattatsu shogai Kenkyu (Studies in Developmental Disabilities)*. Vol. 16, No. 2, pp. 35-39. Nihon Bunka Kagakusha.
24) The following publication was corrected and revised for this section: H. Katoda (2011). "Sueden ni okeru shisetsu kaitai to chiiki seikatsu shien – shisetsu karusurundo no kaitai ni miru sueden shogaisha fukushi kaikaku" (Dissolution of Residential Institutions in Sweden and Community Living – Sweden's Reform of Social Services for the Disabled as Seen through the Dissolution of Carlslund Residential Home). *Rikyodaigaku komyuniti fukushi gakubu kiyo (Bulletin of the College of Community and Human Services, Rikkyo University)*. No. 13, pp. 71-81. 2011.
25) Mehr, H. (1958). *Det nya Carlslund*. Anförande av borgarrådet Hjalmar Mehr vid invigningen av Carlslunds nya vårdavdelningar m.m. den 3 september 1958 (The new Carlslund. Address by city commissioner Hjalmar Mehr at the inauguration of the new wards at Carlslund on 3 September 1985, pp. 5-7. Stockholm: Stockholms stads centralstyrelse för undervisning och vård av psykiskt efterblivna (Stockholm City's central board of education and care of the mentally retarded).
26) SFS 1980:620 Socialtjänstlagen (Act on Social Services). Article 1.

27) Ibid. Article 21.
28) SOU (Statens offentliga utredningar) 1982:46. *Handlingsprogrammet i handikappfrågor (Handicap program for handicap questions).*
29) SFS 1985:569 Lag om införande av lagen om särskilda omsorger om psykiskt utvecklingsstörda m.fl. (Introductory act on special services for mentally retarded and others).
30) Omsorgskommittén (The committee on special services).
31) SOU 1991:46. *Handikapp, Välfärd, Rättvisa* (Handicap, Welfare, Justice). p. 249.
32) SOU 1992:52. *Ett samhälle för all* (Society for all).
33) SFS 1993:387 Lag om stöd och service till visa funktionshindrade (Act concerning support and services for persons with certain functional impairments).
34) SFS 1993:388 Lag om införande av lagen om stöd och service till visa funktionshindrade (Introductory act concerning support and services for persons with certain functional impairments).
35) Ibid. Article 6.
36) The process from the birth of Carlslund residential home to its dissolution is based mainly on the following two publications.
Katoda, Hiroshi (1992). *Sueden no chiteki shogaisha to nomaraizeshon (People with Intellectual Disabilities in Sweden and Normalization).* Gendai Shokan. (Chapter 2: pp. 58-75).
Ericsson, K (2002). *From Institutional Life to Community Participation.* Acta Universitatis Upsaliensis: Uppsala Studies in Education 99 (Chapter 1: pp. 15-32).
37) Gunnarsson, V. (1989). Så tillkom och utvecklades Carlslunds vårdhem (The establishment and development of Carlslund residential home). In: Projekt handikapprörelsens historia (Project History of Disability Movement) (ed.) (1989). *Handikapp historia seminarium 1989: Begåviningshandikappades historia.* (The history of persons with an intellectual disability) Arbetarrörelsens arkiv och bibliotek (Labour Movement Archives and Library).
38) From 1986 onwards, group homes (grupphem) in Sweden were called gruppbostard (community group dwellings). The term group home was changed in response to statements by people with intellectual disabilities for whom the word conjured up images of residential institutions (known as care homes or vårdhem) and who pointed out that group homes within residential institutions were not the same as living in the community. The author, however, has deliberately used the term "community group home" here to make it easier for the reader to understand.

39) Ericsson, K. et al. (1983). *Avvecklingsplan för ett vårdhem* (An institutional closure plan). Psykisk utvecklingshämning nr2 (Mental Retardation No.2).

40) Projekt för avveckling av Carlslund och Klockbacka (1981). *Plan för Carlslunds och Klockbackas avveckling* (An institutional closure plan of Carlslund och Klockbacka). Stockholms läns landsting omsorgsnämnden (Stockholm County Council Care Committee).

41) Stockholm County was the first place in Sweden to categorize community group homes by type. The statements here are based on the document below, but now there are diverse forms of community group homes and therefore group homes are not categorized in this way anymore. In particular, it is no exaggeration to say that the provision of a large, functional living space in group homes built for 4 people greatly changed the concept of the group home.

Hellqvist, L. (1982). *Inackorderingshem, bostadsgrupper, vårdhem* (Boarding house, group home, institution). Stockholm läns landsting (Stockholm County Council).

42) Katoda, Hiroshi (1986). "Shogaisha fukushi ni aratana nagare (jo) (ge)" (A New Trend in Social Services for the Disabled (vol. 1) (vol. 2)). Distributed via *Kyodo News*. 1986.10.

43) The work by Ericsson published in 2002 is as shown below. This section consists of quotations and a summary of the contents of Chapter 1 (pp. 15-32) from the same.

Ericsson, K, 2002, *From Institutional Life to Community Participation*. Acta Universitatis Upsaliensis: Uppsala Studies in Education 99.

44) Omsorgsnämnden (Care Committee) (1975). *Carlslunds framtida vårdinriktning* (The future direction for care at Carlslund). *Memo*. Stockholm: Stockholms läns landsting (Stockholm County Council). 1975-11-17.

45) cf. op. cit. (Projekt för avveckling av Carlslund och Klockbacka (An institutional closure plan of Carlslund och Klockbacka), 1981).

Chapter 3
Deinstitutionalization and Community Living in Japan

Section 1 **Social Welfare Policies for the Disabled and Deinstitutionalization and Community Living in Japan**

The quality of a country's legislation on social services for the disabled is a good indication of the state of those services. In the case of Japan, the current laws in force are the Services and Supports for Persons with Disabilities Act and the Comprehensive Welfare Act for Persons with Disabilities, which when implemented in the near future will replace the former.

The Services and Supports for Persons with Disabilities Act was enacted by the National Diet on October 31, 2005, consecutively implemented from April 1, 2006 and implemented in full force from October 1 of the same year. Although it was intended to be the newest legislation, it will be renewed from April 2013. This will not be a complete overhaul, however, as the ideology behind it as well as the objectives and their content follow the existing law. Concerning the issue of deinstitutionalization, for example, the current Services and Supports for Persons with Disabilities Act promotes "relocation to the community" for certain users while still retaining residential institutions. This policy differs fundamentally from deinstitutionalization, which aims to abolish institutions and consolidate and improve the quality of community based supports and services.

Similarly, the Comprehensive Welfare Act for Persons with Disabilities, which will replace the former, will continue to pursue the same "community relocation" policy and perpetuate Japanese-style "deinstitutionalization". The nature of this Act can thus be assessed by examining the content designated in the Services and Supports for Persons with Disabilities Act and the degree to which the Ministry of Health, Labour and Welfare has incorporated in the new Act the Proposals for the Framework of the Comprehensive Welfare Act for Persons with Disabilities (hereunder Framework Proposals) submitted in September 2012 by the Subcommittee on Comprehensive Welfare,[1] which was established as an arm of the Council for Promotion of Disability System Reform in April of the same year.

1. Various Issues Concerning the Services and Supports for Persons with Disabilities Act

The content of the Services and Supports for Persons with Disabilities Act represented a major reform that unified social services formerly separated into physical, intellectual or mental disabilities, and replaced this system with one in which services were categorized by the level rather than the type of disability. From April 2006, the "benefit principle" system was introduced under which users were as a general rule obliged to pay ten percent of the costs for the social and medical services they received. From October of the same year, the transition to the new system, which consisted of the classification of disability levels, review committees for determining grants, the provision of nursing care and training grants, and the provision of services by community welfare service operators, had begun.[2] Concerning the reforms implemented under the Services and Supports for Persons with Disabilities Act, Okabe noted that they "leave the user's right to receive benefits just as weak as before, while seeking a solution in mandatory state liability based on the premise of a stronger system for managing (controlling) allowances." "Judging from the current situation at least, the shift in focus under 'consolidated social services for the disabled' is about 'ensuring the continuation of the system', by which is meant securing the financial resources for social services for the disabled and ensuring the discretionary power of the Ministry of Health, Labour and Welfare. Moreover, rather than respecting the autonomy and the rights of the system user, this 'conversion to a system that supports independence' imposes on the disabled the burden of paying for benefits, using the principles of self-determination and personal responsibility as justification." "The Act concludes that the concept of 'independence' is essentially 'independence that precludes the need for autonomy', while the main goal of 'support' is 'independence that precludes the need for support' through training that develops the individual's ability to work." "The reforms," Okabe declares, "seek to deconstruct the meaning of 'independence' and 'support'."[3] The following statement by Onoue and Yamamoto would seem to corroborate this point of view. "Looking at the situation after implementation of the Act, the impact of the issues that initially caused concern is even graver than expected. That impact is spreading and can be seen starkly in the lives of the disabled living in the community."[4] With this Act, they declared, social services for the disabled had taken a significant step backwards.

Concerning the "benefit principle" introduced with the adoption and implementation of the Services and Supports for Persons with Disabilities Act, Aizawa criticized the Ministry of Health, Labour and Welfare for using it as a means to secure revenue. "In the first place," he states, "it is the disabled who on behalf of the rest of us bear the risk of disability inherent to any society. Therefore, to ask them to also bear the economic burden of their disability is in principle wrong… The cost of social services for the disabled should be borne through taxation by those who have avoided disability and by corporations."[5]

The Services and Supports for Persons with Disabilities Act has had a major impact on social services for the disabled and has been the subject of numerous commentaries in many research journals and publications produced by organizations in the social welfare field. Here, let me introduce two of the perspectives presented in these commentaries. The first perspective, presented by Iwasaki, "questions the value of independent living support". Iwasaki was critical of the concept of "independence" on which the Services and Supports for Persons with Disabilities Act was based and claimed that the "independent" living support measures defined therein "run counter to our history which has enriched and diversified the meaning of independence. One cannot help but fear that the term will be compressed into a single value." The concept of independence as presented in the Act, he insisted, must be reviewed. "The positive value of support for independent living can only be discovered through the continued creation of a shared world enriched by the perspectives of people from diverse positions."[6]

The second perspective is the argument presented by Sato in the 2005 Japanese Society for the Study of Social Welfare Policy and Theory Forum (Section 1: Examining 20 Years of Welfare Policies). Sato began by pointing out that "scholars of social welfare policies for the disabled exerted hardly any, or perhaps no influence at all, on the legislation process for the Services and Supports for Persons with Disabilities Act, even though the Act represented the greatest revision and transition in Japanese postwar welfare policies for the disabled."[7] There were, he wrote, five studies on welfare policies for the disabled that should have been able to influence the debate, namely, "a study aimed at improving statistics on disabilities", "a study on the concept of independence", "a debate on the issues, which was based on proper studies implemented by scholars on living conditions, livelihood, and international comparisons of welfare systems", "a study on the definition and recognition of disability (qualification for receiving benefits) that objectively grasped the needs", and "a fundamental review of income security, including employment". "If a framework were developed for providing services based on needs, charging the users ten percent of the costs would no longer be necessary. In fact, it would become an obstacle."[8]

In the document mentioned earlier, Okabe wrote, "When formulating the next social services system for the disabled, a true solution to these problems will require the reorganization of this use/payment system based on the three patterns of social assistance, as well as the development of a social service system for users who desire autonomy over their care. The latter would be based on the user-negotiated model and incorporate direct payments for personal assistance. Measures would be needed to prevent instability or rigidity in the financing system for autonomous social services, for which the scale of funding is comparatively low."[9]

As can be seen, the Services and Supports for Persons with Disabilities Act was launched with many unresolved issues. Naturally, evaluations were mixed. "Although some aspects of the legislation can be praised, such as its attempt to unify disability policies and to resolve at a single stroke long-pending issues such as the elimination of long-term hospital stays, the promotion of discharge from mental hospitals, relocation from residential homes to the community, and the consolidation of community living supports to facilitate the same," it was anticipated that many problems would occur "because there was far too little time to properly examine unification".[10] For this reason, many publications criticized the Act.

But what did Ozawa mean by the statement "to resolve at a single stroke long-pending issues"? According to him, the unification of measures for the disabled meant "integrating all measures for institutions dedicated to the different types of disability into three systems of services, namely, nursing care grants, training and other grants, and community-based welfare service businesses." Up until this time, integration of social service systems "could not be easily achieved for various reasons."[11] What made this integration possible, he states, was "the view that institutions are a collection of individuals using a combination of services (and at the same time a collection of individual services)". "By dismantling existing combinations and creating a variety of service combinations, in theory it should be possible to quite easily dissolve the existing institutional system" and thereby effect "a major paradigm shift".[12]

There were some who actively sought to exploit this paradigm shift. Sone stated "It can be said that the principle of the Services and Supports for Persons with Disabilities Act is to create a society of 'independence and coexistence'. To support independent living is to support self-determination. To support self-determination, it is necessary not only to unify the former service system, which was divided according to type of disability, but also to aim for a society of inclusion in which all people, regardless of whether or not they have disabilities grow, learn, work and live together." and that "The purpose of counseling services, community-based welfare service businesses and councils for community living should not be simply to conduct those services. Rather these services should be used as tools to build a society in which it is possible for all people to coexist in the same town in the way that they choose".[13] Shimizu makes the same point that the objective is to "dismantle and rebuild the structure of social services for the disabled and return the subject, the person who is here, now, to the community, and, with these people as the protagonists, to work together in structural and productive activities that create a new way of living." In that sense, the Services and Supports for Persons with Disabilities Act should be seen as "containing the mechanism of potential for the recovery of each individual's value as a human being."[14]

On the other hand, the Act "in reality confronted major issues"[15] and the situation forced those directly involved to tragically yet bravely resolve that "from the perspective of those in the field, all we can do is work together steadily to create a life in the community."[16] The disabled, for whom there was no escape from this reality, were not "asking to fly to the moon or travel around the world but just to live daily life in a way that is true to who we are", and they longed for a system capable of supporting "the aspirations of those who wish to live their lives with dignity".[17] The wishes of the disabled themselves demonstrated that while the Services and Supports for Persons with Disabilities Act did deserve some recognition, in reality, the disabled themselves were still confronted by many unresolved issues and that without addressing that reality, no progress could be made.

The new services system set forth in the Services and Supports for Persons with Disabilities Act replaced the previous system, which was more complex. The Act reorganized existing measures for institutions into daytime activities and in-residence support and established three types of service system for all daily activities, namely nursing care grants, training and other grants, and community-based welfare service businesses. In-residence supports consisted of either admission to an institution or in-home support services (care homes, group homes, welfare homes).[18] Existing residential institutions, which were separated into those for adults with physical disabilities, intellectual disabilities, and mental disabilities, as well as for children with disabilities and medical welfare institutions for children with severe physical and mental disabilities, were to switchover to the new service system by 2011.[19] Critics of the Act noted problems with both in-residence services and day care centers, which were the base for community living activities and daily life, including limitations on continuous use, management problems in welfare service businesses, the heavy burden on users, reduced flexibility in personnel distribution, and lower quality.[20] In addition, personalized support plans and care management for the disabled, both of which are essential for community living, were inadequate, and there was a demand for a comprehensive support system for community living.[21]

"As the principle of a fixed rate for users' fees generated a great deal of criticism even before the Act was implemented, various measures were taken to reduce the burden such as exemptions for certain individual users, exemptions for social services corporations, supplementary benefits for residents of institutions, and reductions in the meal fees for day care centers."[22] Many people, however, felt that the "benefit principle" should be abolished entirely on the grounds that the nursing care grants (rehabilitative care/living care) set forth in the new service system "are the foundation that supports the participation of the disabled in society" and as such the costs "should be paid for according to the consumer's capacity depending on his or her lifestyle and participation at each life stage."[23] Furthermore, "medical payments for services and supports for people with disabilities, which consist of psychiatric outpatient treatment, medical rehabilitation, and rehabilitative treatment for children," essentially "place the burden of payment for benefits on the disabled in order to cut medical disability costs... and discourage the disabled from having medical exams."[24] As such, this provision drew severe criticism on the grounds that "forcing people to bear costs just because they have a disability" is "against the constitution".[25]

Shimizu spoke passionately about community living, declaring that regardless of whether or not a person has a disability, or whether it is mild or severe, and no matter where a person lives or what he or she does, "no one can ever be the 'subject' of welfare services, but rather each person exists 'here and now' as an irreplaceable being of inestimable value, spinning their aspirations for human potential within their particular situation."[26] "The development of social services for the disabled," Shimizu insisted, "is no longer about providing care for or rehabilitating such people. It is not simply about providing services or taking care of someone... The future direction of social services for the disabled is nothing other than building communities in which these people are the main actors."[27] From Shimizu's perspective, the crucial question was whether or not the new service system, which represented the crux of the Services and Supports for Persons with Disabilities Act, provided "valuable services" to "valuable people". He was also questioning the nature of "valuable services". To quote Sone, the nature of these services was none other than "building a society where self-determined support is possible."[28] In Shimizu's words, this was expressed as "a grand movement towards new community living through the creation of user-centered plans based on the individual's aspirations and a circle of support, and through a community network that takes as its standard 'counseling support' and 'community living support councils'."[29]

Although Sone et al thought highly of the principles underpinning the Services and Supports for Persons with Disabilities Act, they pointed out that "it is essential to reassess the conventional framework of gathering the disabled in one place in order to provide services and to build a new framework for providing necessary supports in the regular spaces of child care, school education, the workplace and the home."[30] For this purpose, "it is desirable that counseling services, community-based welfare service businesses and community living support councils collaborate towards 'independence and coexistence', the concepts of community building, and ensure the coherence of support services."[31] Shimizu also declared that, while making full use of the various systems and their interrelatedness, we should "aim for complete deinstitutionalization, promote the development of civil action within community relations", "and aim to establish a social valuation program that confirms the existence of each individual and involves the entire community."[32] It is also true that while acknowledging the passion and enthusiasm of Sone, Shimizu and others, many people pointed out the desperate reality.

Katsumata introduced the results of various studies and commented on the "importance of expanding the concept of securing income to include securing lifestyle".[33] "By setting an upper limit to the cost borne by the user based on household income, the Services and Supports for Persons with Disabilities Act created the scenario in which two persons with the same disability would pay a different user fee due to different household conditions". Katsumata proposed the perspective that "If it is possible to estimate 'the cost caused by having a disability', then it should be possible to estimate the cost for different types of household and indicate the minimum standard of living for non-handicapped people." "When we can consider the cost of a disability and construct a system to secure an income to compensate that cost, we will for the first time be able to establish a fair fee."[34] She further stated that "When considering pertinent issues, people with disabilities need to expand their thinking to encompass the issue of income disparity, and participate in the debate on the same footing as the non-handicapped but from a different starting line."[35]

It was also necessary to carefully examine the classification of services by level of disability, because this, too, affected all aspects of daily life. Ishida noted that "there is much dissatisfaction and, in general, the system of determining disability classifications, including the quality of the examiners, is unpopular. But as there is no use in complaining, people gradually grow accustomed to these unfair conditions and try to adjust as best they can within the system."[36]

The Services and Supports for Persons with Disabilities Act also had a major impact on recreation and leisure activities, which are intended to enrich daily life. Baba, who surveyed the state of overnight trips implemented by residential institutions for the disabled concluded that "compared to before, it has clearly become difficult to maintain the same quality or frequency of trips, which were one form of recreation, due to changes in welfare policies for the disabled or due to shortages of funds on the part of local governing bodies. The same trend is evident in other recreational activities."[37] Sonoda observed a regression "in the presence of recreation in the concrete content of supports"[38]. This may be yet another manifestation of the impact of the Services and Supports for Persons with Disabilities Act.

2. The Services and Supports for Persons with Disabilities Act and Deinstitutionalization and Community Living

Relocation to the community was one important measure that the Act was trying to promote, a fact verified by the marked increase in study reports on the subject at welfare research conferences and in coverage by academic journals, university bulletins, and magazines published by various organizations. The basic study for the Project to Promote Community Based Group Home Support Measures[39] implemented by the Nihon Group Home Gakkai (Japan Group Home Society), an organization composed of people with disabilities and their supporters, examined this topic at every opportunity, and the study reports are valuable resource materials.

In studying relocation to the community and community living, the following three points must be examined: 1) the nature of the system and management methods required to effectively relocate the disabled to the community and to establish and operate group homes and other community based dwellings; 2) methods of relocation and support that prevent confusion when relocating the disabled from residential homes to the community; and, 3) the community support system required to allow the disabled to settle in the community and participate as local citizens after relocation from residential institutions to group homes and other community based residences. In addition, it is essential that such an examination include studies on the users of the services (the disabled persons), their families and the staff members involved.

In a study on service users, Son sought to elucidate the "process by which users develop autonomy based on independence and self-determination" through a qualitative study on "the process of establishing user autonomy among people with intellectual disabilities as observed in deinstitutionalization in England." Through this study, Son found that after relocation to the community, users "continue to adjust their relationship with staff members through various means and retain their enthusiasm for living independently in the community." Son also noted, however, that "at times their enthusiasm wavered" and identified the following points as future issues for study:

1) Creating opportunities for the disabled to recognize their independence as consumers through experience.
2) Opportunities for learning how to adjust relationships with staff.
3) A critical examination of the image of an independent person with disabilities.[40]

Ryo Suzuki undertook a study focused on the families of the disabled. Referring to previous studies indicating that families of the disabled tended to oppose changes when relocation first began, Suzuki conducted a qualitative study on the "attitudes of families towards relocation of people with intellectual disabilities from residential homes A and B" to identify negative factors in relocation to the community that are still evident today. The study results clearly identified the following factors: 1) reliance on institution based welfare services, 2) anxiety about the limitations of the user's capacity, 3) anxiety about the negative effects on the family, 4) anxiety about community based welfare services, and 5) anxiety about the undemocratic decision-making process.[41] Suzuki also pointed out measures for resolving such issues.

Yasuhiko Tarui et al carried out a study focused on staff members through a questionnaire survey on "the relationship between the content of supports and the pattern of orientation towards deinstitutionalization among the staff employed by residential homes for the intellectually disabled" and sought to clarify this relationship through statistical analysis. As a result, he found that:

> when staff members confront the issue of deinstitutionalization, they are clearly aware, despite some internal conflict, of the need to ensure the quality of specialized support services as well as the need to aim for a normal environment that avoids unnecessary institutionalization and values independence (autonomy). At the same time, they viewed fundamental issues related to supports, such as normalization and integration in the community, as a question of the quality of comprehensive supports rather than judging them solely within the framework of the person's living environment, that is, as simply an issue of 'residential home versus the community,' and this recognition was reflected in their actions.[42]

As seen above, it was thought that the ideal form of relocation and community living could be identified by clarifying the quality and state of services along with the users', family and staff members' awareness, attitudes and decision-making processes, which impacted the services, through surveys on the subjects of relocation and community living supports, their families and staff members.

Deinstitutionalization (de-hospitalization) sought "to escape the evils of institutions,"[43] and the movement was sparked by the "spreading current of normalization which demanded social reform that 'ensured a normal life for people with disabilities and, at the same time, recognized that a truly normal society was one in which people lived together regardless of whether they had a disability or not.'"[44] The results of various studies "have made it clear that small scale homes as opposed to large scale residential institutions segregated from the community, and independent living apartments as opposed to life in a group home, provide more opportunities for self-management. The results also verified the importance of deinstitutionalization measures."[45]

But what were the "evils of institutions" to which Son referred? And what were the effects on those involved of the deinstitutionalization measures undertaken in Scandinavia and North America from the late 1960s? There is no need to review the history in detail. Many documents were written on the experiences of residents in residential homes. One of these is *Chiteki shogaisha ga nyushoshisetsu de wa naku chiiki de kurasu tame no hon* (A Book for People with Intellectual Disabilities for Living in the Community Instead of in Residential Homes) published by People First Higashi Kurume. The introduction begins with the following experiences voiced by people with disabilities who lived in residential homes:

> "When I was a child, I wanted to live with my parents, but they put me in a home."
>
> "I don't remember doing anything bad, but they decided to send me to an institution."
>
> "It was like a prison; everything about our life was controlled. I wanted to go out into society but the staff wouldn't let me. They kept saying 'you can't do anything on your own.' 'Wait until you learn to do it yourself.'"[46]

These words from the disabled, who continue to question those who supported and created residential homes on the grounds of social policy, are weightier than any others. It is unclear, however, how much those who were striving to shoulder to shoulder with the disabled really listened to what the disabled had to say. Son did note that ordinary staff members "experience inner conflicts" as they implement deinstitutionalization measures and that they come to demand deinstitutionalization as well.[47] During the process of deinstitutionalization, "as staff repeatedly experience the unforeseen, they begin to see the users as 'people' like themselves...and they also come to recognize the differences between themselves as people without disabilities and the users who have disabilities... This generates empathy for the users and the environment within which they are placed, and also leads to awareness of differences between the users. By discovering what they share in common, and how they differ from the users, staff members become aware of the users' individuality. This motivates them to support the users to express that individuality and results in work satisfaction."[48]

The users, meanwhile, although aware that there are staff members who struggle with such questions in their daily work, have a strong desire for community living and independence. In their own words:

> "I wanted to go out into society."
> "I wanted to decide and do things for myself."
> "It would be better to let us make relationships with people in the community."
> "Wouldn't it be better to be freely involved in the community?"
> "Let's get out into the community."
> "We'll try hard, too."[49]

While we strive to respond to the desires of the disabled, the reality is still difficult. Community living does not always mean the independence the disabled imagine, and wherever the term "support" is used, there lie many factors that can become obstacles to independence because the reality (human relations) does not always meet their expectations of "when I can do something, I don't have to worry because I can ask someone" or "if I can't do something I can ask the caregiver to help."[50] For example, Suzuki found that "opportunities to make decisions on where to live, who to live with, employment, finances, health, etc., are clearly restricted as compared to opportunities to decide such trivial matters related to daily life as the menu or how to use one's allowance. Even when living in the community, opportunities for the disabled to manage their own affairs are restricted compared to society in general."[51] Suzuki also found that "while there are differences depending on the type of home with regards to matters concerning privacy, preferences, daily schedules, and outings, when it comes to menu, finances, work, health, sex, place of residence, and co-habitants, the degree of control exercised by the disabled is comparatively low regardless of the type of residence."[52]

As can be understood from the above, "Deinstitutionalization does not simply mean moving one's place of residence from the institution to the community", but rather it demands that "the users, as members of the community in which they live, participate in the community. For this, they need services, and the nature of those services must change from uniformed group treatment to user-centered support based on the individual's right to self-determination."[53]

Supporters are indispensable to community living, and the quality of community life changes dramatically depending on the nature of the support provided. Hironiwa offered the following perspective on care management for community living: "People (and agencies) involved in the support of service consumers with disabilities should begin by making sure that care management, the skills of support counselors and the activities of welfare service businesses lead to the independence of the service consumers. The capacity to be flexible in the provision of supports will be necessary in achieving the immediate objectives of 1) understanding the essence of care management and widely applying it; 2) improving the skills of support counselors, whose qualifications will be a guide of counseling work; and, 3) allowing the users to live as members of the community."[54] Hironiwa's theory of care management, however, appears to differ slightly from Son's "user-centered support based on each individual's right to self-determination." Son stated that "deinstitutionalization means de-professionalizing support. Accordingly, returning choice and control over one's lifestyle to the user of the services is an important issue."[55]

But what is support that is not controlled by experts? It is difficult to find the perfect answer, but the six points identified by Kishida as "approaches that should be valued in community living support" provide a useful reference. These are:

1) "It's all right to be different" (Cling to self-determination in pursuit of being one's true self. What really matters is whether the user is satisfied and his or her dignity is protected. To support the user to maintain his or her lifestyle.);
2) "Insist on being in the community." (It's better to experience a certain amount of difficulty in life and in one's work or activities. It's important for there to be problems.);
3) "Don't worry. Things will turn out all right." (You don't have to be superman or do everything yourself. Just do what you enjoy doing and leave the things you are not good at to those who are. Don't let yourself be manipulated by information.);

4) "Ordinary social experiences." (Ordinary social experiences are desperately lacking. Leisure supports are extremely effective for accumulating such experiences. Enrichment of free time serves as a barometer of the quality of a person's life.);
5) "Make what isn't already there." (The stance of creating what is lacking is essential for building a lifestyle that suits each individual's needs. If we build a network of supports in society, the power of supports is limitless.); and,
6) "Support capacity" (Whether or not a person can live in the community or be independent depends not only on the severity of the person's disability but on the capacity of the person's supporters and their community.)[56]

Can we stop seeing ourselves as experts and adopt Kishida's approach to providing support? Could we even adopt the approach set forth by supporters of People First Higashi Kurume below?

> The disabled seek to live as ordinary people; they are pursuing happiness, for themselves, for their fellows, as if to shake off past sufferings, confronting daily difficulties and loneliness in order to seize back their lives of which they have been robbed. Supporters of the disabled, inspired by the overwhelming force of this movement, can contribute to these actions by working with the disabled on every aspect, drawing on their own life experience, however limited, and supporting the disabled as they search for answers.[57]

If such an approach were to be applied to and come to permeate community living, surely the nature of social services for the disabled and of society itself would change dramatically.

Many people with disabilities in advanced welfare states now live in ordinary housing in the community. The current issue, however, is how to support them to make relationships with local people and participate in community life. Without appropriate support after relocation, there is a danger of re-institutionalization (mini-institutionalization). In fact, if we look at the lives of the individuals who have left institutions, the reality for many is that they have merely changed their place of residence to the group home where customs and ways of thinking fostered by the institution remain in place. Those involved in support have unconsciously transplanted the structural issues and concepts inherent to the residential institution to the community, continuing to control the residents and obstruct self-determination and leaving many problems that still need to be addressed. This tradition will not simply fade away on its own over time. It is a trend that will continue indefinitely without being recognized, unless the disabled take action. Those involved in their support have also internalized institutional customs. We must learn to listen to the thoughts and wishes of the disabled and ask ourselves how to establish an effective system that will lead to the outcome they desire. We also need to make rules and lobby to make it possible for everyone to live a normal life in the community. We must consider the problem of policies for the disabled and the nature of support from this perspective and construct a user-centered system of community living support as soon as possible.

3. The Framework Proposals and the Comprehensive Welfare Act for Persons with Disabilities

Up to this point, we have examined the various problems concerning the Services and Supports for Persons with Disabilities Act based on documents from fiscal 2006 and 2007. No major change occurred in the realm of social action or in the content of the system in 2008 or 2009. In September 2009, hopes were greatly raised with the unprecedented victory of the Democratic Party and the new Cabinet established under Yukio Hatoyama that consisted of a coalition of the Democratic Party, the Social Democratic Party and the People's New Party. This sign of political reform, however, proved to be short-lived.

In 2006, the same year that the Services and Supports for Persons with Disabilities Act was implemented (April), the United Nations adopted the Convention on the Rights of Persons with Disabilities (hereunder the Convention).[58] The government of Japan supported its adoption but has yet to ratify it after it officially came into effect in May 2008 on the grounds that Japan's domestic laws are not yet ready. Because it contains many items that conflict with the content of the Convention, the above Act falls into the category of laws that 'are not ready'. Despite the Convention's clearly stated purpose "to promote, protect and ensure the full and equal enjoyment of all human rights and fundamental freedoms by all persons with disabilities, and to promote respect for their inherent dignity,"[59] the Japanese government issues "Disability Passbooks" to the disabled, has adopted a system that classifies people by the degree of disability, controls the amount of service grants, allows disparities in community living support services between cities, towns and villages, charges for benefits, and undertakes discriminatory relocation. While all of these measures are implemented to fulfill the Act's stated goal of enabling "persons (adults) and children with disabilities to live independent daily or social lives according to their respective abilities and aptitudes" (Article 1, Services and Supports for Persons with Disabilities Act), the content obviously contradicts the United Nations Convention on the Rights of Persons with Disabilities.

In fact, a lawsuit was filed against the Services and Supports for Persons with Disabilities Act on the grounds that the general rule charging the disabled ten percent of the support costs was unconstitutional. In on January 7, 2010, "The plaintiffs throughout Japan, the defense counsel, and the Ministry of Health, Labour and Welfare accepted the court's final decision... Akira Nagatsuma, the Minister of Health, Labour and Welfare, expressed regret at having 'deeply injured the dignity of the disabled' and promised to switchover to a new system by August 2013."[60] In anticipation of this transition, the Council for Promotion of Disability System Reform (hereunder the Council for Reform) was established. The Council structure was highly unusual in that it was headed by a person with disabilities and more than half of its members belonged to organizations for the disabled or had disabilities. (In reality, of course, this kind of structure should really be the norm.) The Council for Reform established a Subcommittee on the Abolition of Discrimination and a Subcommittee on Comprehensive Welfare. The former commenced debate on revision of the Basic Act for Persons with Disabilities while the latter commenced discussions for drawing up a new law to replace the Services and Supports for Persons with Disabilities-Act. In September 2011 at its 35th meeting and after wide ranging debate, the Subcommittee on Comprehensive Welfare submitted its Proposals for the

Framework of the Comprehensive Welfare Act for Persons with Disabilities (hereunder Framework Proposals), which contained many of the ideas and aspirations of the disabled themselves. These proposals were reviewed by the Ministry of Health, Labour and Welfare and the government parties, after which the Council for Reform, having finished its designated role, was disbanded at the end of 2011.

The Framework Proposals were equivalent to a report on the findings of a national commission and as such they should have been honored, allocated a budget, and implemented. This, however, did not happen. The Proposals was made up of the "points" and "proposals" outlined below (quoted from Reference 2 prepared by the Council for Reform):[61]

The 6 Points of the Comprehensive Welfare Act for Persons with Disabilities
(1) The same equality and fairness as for citizens without disabilities
(2) Elimination of gaps and blanks
(3) Correction of disparities
(4) Resolution of social problems that require urgent attention
(5) Support services that fit the needs of the user
(6) Guarantee of a stable budget

Framework Proposals for Welfare for the Disabled (the relationship to other laws and fields has been omitted)
(1) Ideology, purpose and scope of the law
   Realization of a society of coexistence where the presence or absence of disabilities forms no barrier
   A shift from being the subject of care to the wielder of rights and from the medical model to the social model in the concept of disability
   The right to lead an independent life in the community
(2) The scope of disability (persons with disabilities)
   Persons with disabilities (including children) who are the subject of the Comprehensive Welfare Act for Persons with Disabilities are as stipulated in the

Basic Act for Persons with Disabilities

Physical and mental functional impairments include functional impairments accompanied by chronic disorders

(3) Selection and Decisions (Grant Decisions)

A new grant decision framework to replace the classification by level of disability

Respect for the wishes, etc. of the user based on the service use plan

Guarantee of sufficient grant funds through consultation and adjustment

Establishment of a council system and appeal

(4) Support (Services) System

Construction of a support system based on the Convention on the Rights of Persons with Disabilities that makes community living possible and is centered on the autonomy of the disabled persons

Composed of supports provided under a common national framework and supports provided in response to local conditions

(5) Relocation to the Community

Clearly state in the Act that the nation will promote relocation to the community to eliminate admissions to hospitals or institutions for social convenience rather than need.

Formulate and implement legal measures for relocation programs and community based support

Use peer supporters

(6) Prepare a Base for Community Living

Legislate the formulation of a 10-year strategy for the establishment of a community base for systematic promotion of the plan

Municipal and prefectural governments indicate the disability welfare service plan while the national government indicates the basic policy and implementation plan

Establish community living support councils

(7) Cost Borne by Users

Costs for food and utilities will be borne by the user.

Supports necessitated by a disability will in general be free but those users who have a high income will bear some of the costs according to their ability to pay

(8) Counseling Support

Those eligible for counseling support include persons with disabilities who are already receiving support, those who potentially need support, and their families.

Continuous coordination of comprehensive supports for all problems faced by persons with disabilities

Establish a multi-faceted counseling support system

(9) Protection of Rights

Protection of rights encompasses all petitions, consultations, uses, and appeals from persons with disabilities who desire, or are using, support.

Establishment of an ombudsperson system

Prevention and early detection of abuse

(10) Securing Remuneration and Personnel

As a general rule remuneration for support provided to users will be paid by the day, that for project management will be paid by the month and that for care in the home will be paid by the hour.

Remuneration will be a standard, payable amount that is considered appropriate wages and allows welfare workers to take pride in their work and have a vision of the future

Setting aside my own personal views on the content, the Framework Proposals, which summarized the consensus of the disabled and the other members of the Council for Reform, and its contents were unprecedented and highly significant. If the content of those proposals had been realized within the legal system, Japan would have moved far closer to becoming an advanced welfare state. The Ministry of Health, Labour and Welfare, however, as if it foresaw the weakness of the ruling Democratic Party and the coming political confusion, arose to obstruct it. Twice the Ministry submitted pessimistic comments, and in the end, the majority (probably close to ninety percent) of the content was never realized. In March 2012, a final token meeting was held and the Council was brought to an end.

The content of the new law drawn up by the Ministry of Health, Labour and Welfare was almost identical to the Services and Supports for Persons with Disabilities Act. Only the name was changed, becoming the Comprehensive Welfare Act for Persons with Disabilities. With regards to the issue of deinstitutionalization, it became a "community relocation" policy that retained residential institutions, an approach that is fundamentally different from what is recognized as "deinstitutionalization" in the rest of the world.

4. From the Era of the Disabled as a Consumer of Services to the Era of Consumer Control

The legal system of a country is the barometer indicating the maturity of its social services. As such, fairness and efficiency are required. Because the laws are intimately involved with finite sources of revenue, they do not always match the degree of satisfaction in the quality of life for those concerned. Even if, however, the legal system was improved and the quality of life was greatly increased, there would be no way of knowing whether or not those concerned were satisfied without listening to what they have to say.

Considerable time has passed since people began talking about the "age of community services and the age of self-advocacy."[62] Each year new publications present the memoirs and histories of people with disabilities and of their supporters who have worked with them, and reports on practical actions supporters have taken. Of these, literature written by the disabled themselves makes us acutely aware of our shameful past, of our history of expelling the disabled from our midst, of our shortcomings and mistakes, our unfairness and immaturity, of just how awful we can be. Through the personal accounts of the disabled we learn that we should examine the true nature of any situation and the true nature of human endeavors. There are many approaches in this world and diverse methods for realizing those approaches. But there is only one truth. Why is it that people have had to suffer so much and struggle their whole lives in order to reach and verify that truth when it is one and the same? Why is it that people must fight so hard to bring to our attention the evils of residential homes, to reject them with loathing and insist on community living, to find a place in the community so that no one ever again will have to experience what they were forced to experience?

Literature authored by people with disabilities has so much to teach us. The book *Teiko no akashi: watashi wa ningyo janai* (Proof of Resistance: I'm Not a Doll) [63] by Kinuko Mitsui is no exception. Mitsui graphically depicts the inhumane conditions she experienced and the reality of social discrimination against the disabled. We cannot ignore the tragedy she experienced. We must not forget the historical facts against which she fought so valiantly, nor let them fade away with time. Her account teaches us what it is to be human, to be a married couple. It teaches us what the word family means and what it means to bear and raise children, to live with a disability, and to live in the community. It goes beyond the issue of disability to inform us of what human relationships should be, how precious it is to live happily as a family, how peaceful our society is, the importance of each of us living as a human being, the fragility, transience and richness of love, the importance of raising children without instilling prejudice and without allowing them to have prejudice, and the difficulty and the importance of creating equal relationships. This single volume is a lesson in the power of the voice of the disabled.

One of the most outstanding representatives of the disabled in recent years is Kimiyo Sato. Looking back on sixteen years of living independently with a ventilator and 24-hour care, she wrote: "A ventilator is like a pair of glasses or a hearing aid. It's part of my body, a tool for living. In no way does this machine force me to constantly confront the fear of death." "To live with a ventilator is a perfectly normal part of my daily life, on the same level as exercising my personal responsibility when deciding what to do with a burnt egg." "I realize that a negative image of having a disbality and a ventilator could be very much like a haunt that our society has created." She concludes her article with this powerful statement: "With my ventilator as my trusty partner, I will live my life in the way that suits who I am, confident that mine is a bright and shining life."[64]

Many of those who live in the age of the disabled as a consumer of services feel the difficulties of coexistence. On the other hand, there are supporters who have always coexisted with the disabled from the time when they were excluded from society to the present. How kind and wonderful they were as they strove to walk side by side with the disabled.

Ikuyoshi Mukaiyachi recorded his memories of Bethel House, the people he met and events that occurred around him. He begins with an episode that perfectly captures the content. "Sitting casually down beside a disabled person who has collapsed in a mud puddle, sharing the powerless of not knowing what to do, then looking at one another and suddenly bursting into laughter at the ridiculousness of the situation—at moments like these I feel the limitless possibilities of life and the power of people with disabilities."[65] In his conclusion, he teaches us the importance of trusting the disabled themselves and how to work closely with them. "And in the midst of the conflicts that arose with those around them and the darkness of a confusion that I myself could not penetrate, the person involved would still work hard to find a way out." Through Mukaiyachi's words we can learn the importance of trying to understand the feelings of the disabled, to imagine "what would I do if that were me?" and "more important than what I would do, to recognize what I would not do."[66] We can find this same tone within the following words: "What I treasured in that daily routine was the fact that they are striving to live now "notwithstanding", and the wisdom to be content with the reality we have been given. And what saved me was the laughter that could be heard at all times from Bethel House."[67]

Sadaharu Nishi focuses on Sakura, a child born to parents with intellectual disabilities. Into this story, he weaves accounts of the people he met and the events he witnessed. Through Sakura's parents, Nishi speaks about sex, love, marriage, pregnancy and child rearing by people with intellectual disabilities. He also frankly shares his dilemma about the gap between ideals and reality and the feelings that threaten to defeat him. But even while laying bare his complex emotions, his internal conflict and over eagerness, he introduces individuals who are attempting to change social values "so that people with disabilities can deepen their relationship with their partners as they live life together."[68] His account is structured in such a way that the unadorned description of his interactions with Sakura and her life convey his powerful sense of purpose. Nishi passionately questions our society, riddled as it is with discrimination and prejudice, and directs his criticism towards our ignorance and insensitivity. The destination to which he is heading is, I believe, "a normal life in the community" and the "meaning of coexistence".

The measures for the organizational reform of Sweden's Grunden Organization also demonstrated the possibility of moving from the era of the disabled as consumers to the era of consumer control. The Grunden Organization "separated from the July 2000 Parents' Association, and formed an independent [social welfare corporation] for the disabled supported by its own financial resources on May 2, 2001. It employed support staff and began to undertake various activities." "People with disabilities are in charge of decision making and management and employ supporters and staff while running various enterprises including media production (newspapers, magazines, radio programs, websites), film production, a coffee shop, recreational activities, human rights protection and the establishment of international networks."[69] The former institution director (now a supporter), Anders Bergström, shared the interesting account below:

> First and foremost, the basis for Grunden is that it is an organization of the disabled. It became independent from the parents organization in 2000 and began operating as an organization for the disabled. The following year, however, we realized that while there were people with disabilities on the board of directors, people in the positions of greatest authority, like myself, were employed. The first to notice this were the directors Anna and David. Three years ago we decided to change this structure. It took three long years after that decision to actually change because at first we thought of employing members with a salary. In order to do that, we needed to spend a lot of time and energy looking for funding from other organizations and financial resources. In the end, we could not obtain the funding we needed, and therefore we reached the conclusion that more important than providing a salary was to change the structure. The members could live on their pension and allowance. Second, we studied and surveyed what other organizations of the disabled were actually doing. But we found no good examples. So we decided to make our own structure in which authority was not rested solely in people representing the disabled. It took a long time, but the new organization began operating in January 2005.[70]

Currently, the board of directors (Grunden's highest decision making body) consists of eleven people with disabilities, who oversee an office director and four other office posts. The executive functions formerly performed by Bergström are now performed by five people with disabilities who are assisted by two supporters. Thus the authority and functions previously invested in Bergström have been transferred to the disabled, transforming the organization into one truly run by the disabled for the disabled. Recalling that time, Bergström said:

> I thought it was strange that even though we called it an organization of the disabled, there were no people with disabilities in decision-making positions, and therefore I thought that I should resign from the job. There was no question about this in my mind. Rather I felt very relieved because I thought that it would help increase the overall leadership capacity of the disabled. By resigning, it became possible for many people to take on more interesting and responsible jobs. I had no anxiety about entrusting the work to them. We hired a professional consultant for that purpose and spent time and money on leadership training. In the office where I used to work, two people with disabilities are now working. I just have a small desk and a small computer. The way I work has not changed much since then but if anything happens to the other employees, they now ask the new office members first, not me. That is the biggest change. And also, when documents need signing, I am no longer the one who signs them."[71]

The approach adopted by the Grunden Organization is bound to have a large impact in the welfare field in Japan as well, and I am convinced that both the "age of the disabled as consumers of services" and the "age of consumer control" will lead to the construction of a society of coexistence.

5. In Lieu of a Conclusion

The essence of true welfare, I believe, is to make it possible for all people to live without barriers, without being subjected to discrimination, with a mutual appreciation for diversity, taking pride in each person's unique values and way of life, possessing the right to dignity and freedom of choice, participating in decision making and enjoying the fruits of social development, and it is realized through social services and the way we live our lives (awareness and behavior born from that awareness) while fully utilizing social policies, movements, support activities and methods (knowledge, skill development, etc.). This is the kind of welfare that will lead to "happiness" and "richness of spirit" for all.

The movement for reform of social services for people with disabilities has undergone diverse changes. We are now beginning to see the formation of those concepts and values that are directed at "human dignity" and "full participation and equality", which are the foundation of welfare for the disabled today. Structural changes are also evident in the basic ideology, concepts and principles, such as the normalization principle, that formed the foundation of conventional social services for the disabled. Naturally, the legal system related to welfare for the disabled, the contents of welfare services, the nature of support and the methods of social participation will continue to change. Even if these changes are gradual, it is my ardent hope that these efforts will contribute to building a society where we can all walk together. Regardless of how slow progress towards community living may seem, or how distant consumer control may appear, it is my hope that that era will finally come.

Section 2   The State of Deinstitutionalization and Community Living in Japan

About seven or eight years ago, the author with several other researchers visited A Institution run by A Corporation, which was actively promoting relocation to the community. We stayed for two days to experience what life was like there. By experience I mean that we physically placed ourselves in that environment, observed from an objective perspective the state of living for the users, and recorded that experience. The contents of all our reports were similar and severe in their assessment. The living environment in the residential home for the users as observed by the authors "lacked privacy... Their lifestyle was far from human, and it would be hard to claim that their dignity as human beings was being maintained."[72]

Although these accounts describe the recent situation in a welfare corporation that is quite famous in Japan and is actively promoting relocation, the description resembles far too closely what Bengt Nirje witnessed in the late 1960s in residential institutions in America.

> There is no privacy, and nothing personal is possible. Such wards offer only dehumanizing and impersonal life conditions.[73]

Although the era and the quality of these two institutions differed, they reminded me of what such residential homes were like and inspired me to review and assess the situation, not just in B Corporation's B Institution where I once worked, but also in other residential institutions. I will begin with a brief overview of the situation in residential institutions from the 1970s to the present followed by an assessment. For this review, I have used as a reference the six characteristics of institutions identified in the report[74] from the Swedish Ministry of Health and Social Affairs (1990) quoted in Section 1 of Chapter 2—namely, 1) invisibility, 2) isolation, 3) mechanical and monotonous, 4) intensively managed (no role or aspirations in the community), 5) no connection with society, protective, and 6) no respect for the person's wishes, unequal—to identify the following indicators for assessing whether a disabled person's residence is an institution or not, or, if you would, indicators for assessing whether or not a person is a participating member of society (the community):

1) Measures for community relocation are transparent.
2) The person is living in the community as a member of society.
3) Measures are flexible and can be changed.
4) The person has a role and aspirations in the community.
5) The person has connections with the community and is autonomous.
6) The person's wishes are respected and he/she is equal.

Based on these six indicators, I will examine and evaluate the situation from the 1970s to the present in Japanese residential institutions and the state of community relocation (which is far removed from deinstitutionalization).

1. The State of Deinstitutionalization in and Assessment of B Institution Run by B Corporation

1) From the 1970s to the 1980s

In order to understand the situation of residential institutions in Japan in the 1970s, let me begin by introducing an essay I wrote for the bulletin of residential institution B run by B Corporation at which I used to work. Located in Tokyo, it was established as a public institution in 1972 for 150 residents and subsequently became a social welfare corporation. Rereading my essay now, I realize that it is very subjective and poorly written, but the content does give a clear picture of how a young man in his twenties just out of university viewed the residential institution in which he worked. In 1974, B Institution was a public residential home for children with severe to very severe intellectual disabilities. It boasted not only magnificent buildings but also a full medical staff (30 doctors and nurses), training staff (30 including management), a high proportion of living support staff (210 in the living wards, including the subsection chief, for 150 long-term users and up to 10 short-term users) and office staff (30 including management). It exceeded in scale a certain national facility that was hailed as the best in the Orient. I wrote the following for the bulletin towards the end of my second year working there.

> ...In the institution, many children live together and follow a standard routine controlled by many staff members with differing opinions who treat the children differently. The children appear to have some freedom but they do not. Instead, they are always thwarted by the staff in the name of "protection" and are forced to do things despite having no clue as to why or what they are doing. And this continues their whole life long... We tend to place more emphasis on experience

and regard theory lightly. In the clash of differing experiences, the staff members struggle to reach a consensus. They fight over trivial things, creating rifts between themselves (a frequently occurring phenomenon)... To improve the users' environment, we need to consider whether or not the institution, the people who work at the institution and the children are in the community. It will not work if institution staff members live in the institution. The children cannot meet and make connections with the local people and become integrated into the community if the staff does not live in the community... It is also important that people in the community can freely enter the institution.... The various facilities should be open to the public. If we are going to expand our facilities, whether by building a gymnasium or a sports ground, the additions should be built outside near to the institution so that both local people and children from the institution can access the facilities freely and use them together. A life where all their needs are met inside the institution will just distance the children even further from the community. Likewise I hope that the children will be able to attend the local school with other children in the community as soon as possible...[75]

These opinions were ignored by the management and were never reflected in the operation of the organization. In frustration, I and some of my colleagues decided to make our own magazine with a limited circulation, which we distributed to all the staff. We continued doing this from 1978 to 1979. We published 15 editions of the bulletin until we were no longer able to continue due to having taken on different roles and activities. I expressed my thoughts in many essays in this bulletin from which I introduce the following excerpt from just one of these:

> Why did the children living in B Residence have to come and live here? Why did they have to leave their parents and their siblings to live in an institution?
> Normally, people marry and establish a family. They have children and live a rich and boisterous life...Their relationships within the community may not always be smooth, but still civilization progresses, and even if nuclear families

have become more common, this age old pattern is carried on. While we may experience hardships within a family, yet we still want to participate as a member of that family and of society, and to raise our children and live together under one roof.

Why then must children with disabilities who are born within such a family environment leave their parents and live in an institution? I can think of countless reasons—to overcome their disability, out of educational considerations, to reduce the burden on their parents—but I will not bother to address those here. When I stop to consider whether these reasons really lead to happiness for these children, I am forced to express my doubts.

Are we treating these children who have been separated from their parents with warmth? Are we, as their fellow human beings, offering an environment in A Institution where they can find even a little bit of real happiness? Are we doing our best during every shift, which represents only 8 hours out of the 24-hour cycle of their daily lives? We are charged with the job of creating a rich life for these children. This includes enriching and protecting our own lives, too. Why then does it seem that our feelings for these children don't reach them no matter how hard we try? Or perhaps the truth is that we have abandoned them.

Some children have left the institutions, having given up hope. Others issue us a challenge through "problem behavior" as they fight a lonely battle. What on earth does "home" look like to children who were admitted to an institution without any choice? Living as they do with other severely disabled children, how do they perceive the institution, their parents, their siblings? Isn't this the exact opposite of how they would want to be treated?

Is it justice to deny these children a natural life, one which includes school, going out, and making friends, and to confine them to a small room simply because they have a disability, simply because they need special educational measures? As far as I can see, life in an institution for such children is far from pleasant.[76]

The situation described above continued until the late 1980s when the author left B Institution. I and my colleagues made many attempts to improve the situation. We presented the content of improvement measures and pointed out the problems at every opportunity.[77] Unfortunately, we almost never felt that our efforts were rewarded. I still remember the day I left B Institution. I stood before the users and declared: "I want to work to change society so that there is no longer any need to use B Institution." I have clung to this objective as I continue to explore the meaning of deinstitutionalization and community living at every opportunity.

2) From the 1990s to the Present

As I have not followed what happened in B Institution since I left in April 1986, I introduce here the objective opinions that others have voiced about the institution.

At one point, B Institution conducted an internal reform under the guidance of the management. During the process of developing reform measures, several people were invited on different occasions to speak at the institution. The following statements are from their talks or from letters they sent to the institution director.[78] Please note that these messages are from sixteen years ago.

> There is no color and no greenery in the ward, nor is there any personal space. Is this place really suitable for human beings to live in? I have never seen such a cold institution. I am not saying that prefectural institutions are luxurious. But do they use the funds and staff they have in such a way that they can proudly declare that people are happy here?" (January 1996, N)

> When I saw that day room, I thought how painful this must be for the mothers. It's hard enough to be separated from one's child but they are forced to leave their children in that barren room, just as if they were in a zoo. The users are controlled far more than necessary – 'Key! Key! Key!.' They run for the toilet in their bare feet… It made me very sad. I wept as I left the place, feeling what it must be like for the mothers, for the users… (October 1996, M)

It is clear from the testimonies of N and M that B Institution in the mid-1990s had not changed in terms of its environment or in its treatment of the users since the author worked there from the 1970s to the 1980s.

Referring to the institution's homepage[79] on July 8, 2012, I found that the total capacity as of April 1, 2012 had increased by 10 users (160 long-term plus 10 short-term) with 151 actual users. There were 20 two-person rooms, 31 three-person rooms, and 9 four-person rooms. The total number of staff was 275 (regular 231, part-time 41). Formerly a public institution, it was now run by the Tokyo Prefectural Social Welfare Corporation. Its day services (nursing care services for daily living) had been opened to the community, a rehabilitation counseling section had been established, and 15 people had been relocated to the community by 2008.

According to a third party assessment of social services and user survey results[80], the overall evaluation was positive, with the users (the parents, not the person with the disabilities) responding that they were generally "satisfied". In response to the question, "Do you think the feelings of the users are being respected?" 54% responded "yes" while 36% responded with "neither one nor the other" and 10% said "no". This still indicates, however, that nearly half of the respondents did not necessarily think that the users were satisfied. A similar response was observed for the question, "Is it easy to tell the office (institution) what you are dissatisfied with or what you want?" While 52% said "yes", 36% responded "neither one nor the other", 5% responded "no" and 7% did not respond at all. If we consider the position in which the users and their families were placed, it seems likely that the third party assessment does not accurately represent the lives of the users in the institution, nor how they and their families really feel about it.

3) Overall Assessment

Although only a subjective assessment is possible, from the above information it seems clear that the scale of the institution, the content of the supports it provides, and its environment have not changed greatly since I worked there. In the above mentioned third party assessment of the social services and user survey results, users who responded that it was difficult to tell the office (institution) their complaints or demands commented that "I want more time to walk and move around", "I am worried that there are too few staff. Please think about increasing the number of staff", "I am worried about my child's future (i.e. transferring from the facility for children to the adult facility)," and "I want you to put more effort into keeping the institution clean." Although the number voicing such sentiments may be few, these comments demonstrate that there are parents and relatives who feel the same way that I felt.

2. The Situation in and Assessment of C Institution Run by C Corporation

C Institution run by C Corporation was established in Tokushima prefecture in 1960 and has a capacity of 150 users. It has been covered frequently on TV and in magazines and other media, and the coverage gives the impression that the users' lives are far from normal and very empty. Below I quote directly from the narration of a television documentary aired on September 24, 1998.

> There are 150 men and women living in this institution. [Note: As of July 9, 2012, there were 3 full-time service managers, as well as one service manager who worked at more than one facility, plus 47 full-time and 15 part-time living support staff all of who worked at more than one facility.] The day begins at 6:30 in the morning. The users line up in the hall and wait for the staff to come. Staff members check that the users are up and wake up those who are still asleep...
>
> After breakfast, there's morning assembly from 8:45 at which the users are given instructions. They spend the day following a predetermined schedule. Up at 6:30, bed at 9:00.
>
> Because they spend their day as a large group of 150, the schedule is very detailed...[81]

About two months before the television program was aired, the following article describing conditions in this institution appeared in the Inclusion Japan bulletin. (The article was a training journal written by an intern who spent several days training in a different section of C Institution.)

> (Meals) In the institution where I received training, the staff got mad at the users if they talked during meals, and if the users didn't do what the staff said, they were sent out of the cafeteria. The way of teaching and disciplining the users differed from one staff member to another and also depending on the staff members' mood. Because the institution itself runs according to a schedule, even if some users were still eating, they had to start cleaning up.[82]

> (Bath time) From a little after one o'clock, the users are put into a small bath one after the other in what is called "bath training". Despite the word 'training', the staff members wash the users, and even if some users are capable of washing themselves a little, staff members might insist that they weren't capable and do it for them... When I asked a staff member, 'Do you use this bath when you're on night duty?' I was told, 'How could we? If we used this bath when it's used by so many people, we'd have to go home and wash again to get clean.'... It was like we were washing animals rather than fellow human beings.[83]

> (Relations between staff and users) I saw a staff member make a user hold an ashtray for him while he smoked and knocked the ashes into it...Do the staff members hold an ashtray for the users when they smoke?" "At the morning assembly, the users turn their chairs to face the staff, just as if they were in the army... On holidays, regardless of their wishes, the users are woken up early, made to attend morning assembly and then told by the staff 'don't do anything to bother us.'[84]

The above was discovered because the intern was training in a different section of C Institution and was in a position to freely write a journal. (The section where he was training was undertaking vocational and community living support. Many of residents who were relocated from C Institution were relocated through this section.) The account makes us acutely aware that inappropriate treatment, which could be termed discriminatory, was routine in C Institution.

The latter half of the documentary aired on September 24, 1998 introduced such improvement measures as insisting that the staff refer to the users as "Mister" or "Ma'am" and that the users be given menu choices at meals. In addition, the buildings were in the middle of being rebuilt to improve the living environment (converting living quarters to 2-person rooms). But clearly there was doubt as to whether such measures could successfully eradicate the domineering attitude of the staff or the closed and excessively controlled life so characteristic of institutions

Having witnessed the situation in such institutions, I and others in the field launched an "Institution Reform Project" with students. On the basis of the following understanding, we stayed in C Institution to experience what life was like there and drew up institution reform proposals, the main points of which follow after.[85] We submitted our proposal to the director of C Corporation with a request to apply the suggestions to reform of the institution.

Understanding:

Institutional reform can only be called reform when it solves the structural problems inherent to large-scale institutions, namely, a structure based on the premise of group management that tends to give priority to the working conditions and wishes of the staff, making it difficult to provide individual support. It is only when concrete interventions in the environment are implemented that reform is effective. Superficial reform that preserves the structure causing the 'disease' is meaningless. In that sense, the proposals below must not stop with the reform of C Institution but must extend into social reform, shifting from care provided in residential institutions that combine the residence with the place of daily activity, to personal, humane care that suits each individual's needs and is provided within the community.

Outline of the Institution Reform Proposals:
1) Subdivide the institution and relocate to the community, dispersing functions in the community. Even if the institution retains some of its functions, these should be used as social resources within the community.
2) Subdivide the living wards of the residential institution, reduce the living units to a small, home-like scale with at most 4 to 5 people, and guarantee individual rooms. Actively promote employment and other daily activities in the community while also promoting the establishment of community group homes and independent living.
3) The institution and all other spaces, as well as activities and care of the users, should be user-centered with a high degree of freedom and complete assurance of privacy and non-violence.

Judging from the incidents described in the above accounts, overall C Institution failed to take even a single step beyond the existing insular framework of residential institutions, a reality which can be glimpsed from the report printed in the Inclusion Japan bulletin. Compared to B Institution run by B Corporation, which had a user:staff ratio of 160:275, the ratio at C Institution run by C Corporation was 150:62,[86] making the gap between public and private institutions obvious. Although from the assessment of the protection of rights at C Institution,[87] none of the parents and others involved in the institution appeared to be upset by the conditions they witnessed, we can assume that there were potentially many who did feel some anguish.

3. The State of Deinstitutionalization and Community Living in and Assessment of D Institution Run by D Corporation

D Corporation was established as a private social welfare organization in the Tokai district of Shizuoka prefecture in 1966 by supporters of the philosophy of a Christian couple. As of April 2010, it has developed into a social welfare corporation with 17 offices in 5 districts[88] (support facilities for people with disabilities, 5 enterprises that provide nursing care in the home, children's day service and temporary daytime support, community workshops to promote independent living, after school support programs, communal living nursing care programs with 2 offices serving 5 locations, a residential rehabilitation home, a home for children and adults with severe physical and mental disabilities and an A-style day workshop, 3 counseling support offices, a research center).

D Corporation is striving to free itself from institution-centered measures by providing small-scale living units, separating the place of residence from the place of daily activity, expanding measures for relocating residents from the institution to housing in the community, and implementing measures "aimed at rebuilding the community with people who have intellectual handicaps."[89]

In early December 2010, I visited each office and facility of D Institution for two days to conduct participant observation and offer advice concerning the rebuilding of the rehabilitation facility for people with intellectual disabilities scheduled for fiscal 2011. As a result, I was able to inspect and assess D Corporation's user support services.

D Corporation began as a residential institution and, although it was moderate in size, it still had three residential facilities. For this reason, it was necessary to begin the inspection and assessment of support measures by first looking at the residential institutions as well as the community living support measures implemented by the backup facilities. The following content is based on participant observations during the time spent at the institution. The results likely contain some subjective observations. I strove to examine the facilities from the perspective of how I would feel and think if I lived and worked there as an individual with the "right to pursue freedom and happiness."[90]

1) Residential Rehabilitation Facility (Capacity 50 users, Current number 45: 26 males, 19 females; average age male 50.3, female 52.5; number of staff 25: 1 director, 3 office staff, 1 nurse, 1 nutritionist, 18 living support staff, 1 support assistant)[91]

The door of the institution's central entrance was locked. The 50 users live in 4 independent small-scale wards. The users can enter and leave their own building freely but no one can leave the institution without going through the central exit. Each ward consists of 2 to 3-person rooms but they are not managed independently. Instead staff members are assigned to different wards within the overall personnel placement plan for the entire institution. I was told that if they organized separate shifts for each ward, it would be hard to manage shifts for the entire institution. The advantages of the small-scale ward system did not appear to be sufficiently exploited. Perhaps for that reason, the users seemed rather lifeless. Almost all of the users speak to the staff, seeking communication, but these interactions are short-lived as they earn only a temporary response from staff members. At lunchtime, perhaps due to lack of human resources, the meal scene is far from enjoyable and in fact seems very dreary. Some instructive and controlling behaviors were observed in the staff's treatment of the users.

2) Daily Living Care Office/Community Workshop to Promote Independence

The users were engaged in woodworking and crushing cans. They perform these jobs every day in the same way and do not appear to be enjoying the work. It made me wonder if there was not some other kind of activity they could be doing, one with more variety that would allow each individual to shine, that would allow a more flexible approach and respect the users' wishes more. Some elements of the work environment, such as dust and ash disposal methods, and the one-sided interactions by some of the staff members were also a concern.

3) After School Support Program

The users were mainly just supervised in a confined space, and, perhaps because their charges were children, I noticed that much of the interaction was disciplinary, with the staff giving directions or commands or grabbing the children's arms. I could only pray that such actions did not escalate into inappropriate treatment.

4) Communal Living Support Program (one 4-person space, two 5-person spaces, two 6-person spaces)

The atmosphere here differed from the residential rehabilitation facility. The users looked more cheerful and gave me the impression that those using the communal living support program have a higher level of satisfaction than those in the residential institution. There was one home built within the institution grounds, but considering the purpose of these homes, it should be located outside the institution.

5) Disabled Persons Support Facility (Child user capacity: 20; Current number: 19; 15 males, 4 females, 3 elementary school, 1 junior high school, 7 senior high school students; 8 over age 19. Adult user capacity & current number: 30; 21 males, 9 females; average age: males 43.3, females 42.0; Number of staff: 22; 1 director, 2 office, 10 nurses, child care workers, supporters, 1 psychologist, 4 kitchen staff, 1 care assistant, 3 others)[92]

This was D Corporation's first attempt to create a facility with private rooms for all with just 5 to 6 people composing a single living unit. This new style of residence is designed to protect the privacy of each individual and allow the users to lead a more natural human life. Due to lack of manpower, however, there was not much interaction with staff and the staff seemed to spend all their time doing odd jobs. The staff also seemed to be managing the users. It is doubtful that the users had any meaningful way to spend their free time. I observed many of them wandering aimlessly about the corridor, as if they had nothing to do. The children's section where the users are bursting with energy was mercilessly controlled by the staff, and there were signs that the staff were constantly under stress. Generally speaking, the problems and issues of unit style housing were apparent, and it was clear that relations between the staff and the users were superficial and that the staff members were not aware of all that was going on.

4. Assessment and Future Expectations of the 3 Institutions Run by 3 Welfare Service Corporations

The assessment of the measures adopted by the above institutions based on participant observations and various documents are as follows:

1) Transparency of measures for community relocation: It was hard to call the measures of the three institutions visible transparent.
2) Living in the community as a member of society: The users lived in the institutions, and although they were working, they could not really be called active members of

society.

3) Diversity and freedom: The users of each institution did not exercise freedom in their lives nor were their lives, work or daytime activities varied.
4) Role/expectations in the community: The users of each facility did not really have a role or expectations in the community through the work they performed or the activities in which they were involved.
5) Social relationships and autonomy: The users did not really have a relationship with society or autonomy in their daily lives, work or activities.
6) Respect of the users' wishes and equality: The users' wishes were not respected and they could not be called equal. In fact, there was a possibility that their rights were being abused.

When examining the institutions against the above indicators, the results were apparent. In brief, the results demonstrate that residential institutions obstruct the protection of the users' rights and fail to provide an enriching life. Accordingly, the proposals for institution reform submitted by the Institution Reform Project would not have been very effective. Yet, organizations such as D Corporation were still attempting to undertake reforms, involving the entire organization in these efforts. For any institution, however, the objectives of reform must be to "1. provide smaller-scale living units, 2. expand the choices and freedom of the users, increasing their autonomy and empowerment, 3. make it possible for the users to participate in local community activities and bear a role through which they can fulfill their responsibility as community members,"[93] and "4. separate the place of residence and the place of daily activity".[94]

These four objectives raise many questions (issues). For example, what does it mean to offer smaller-scale living units? What does it mean to expand the users' choices and their freedom? What are autonomy and empowerment? What does it mean to participate and play a role in local community activities (or to fulfill one's responsibility as a member of the community)? What is the separation of residence and workplace? What kind of support conforms to users' needs? What does rebuilding community mean? We must examine each of these questions (issues) and seek answers. A review (examination) of practical steps that have been taken to date is also needed. We need to ask ourselves, for example, whether or not measures implemented in November 2008, such as the attempt to separate the place of residence from the place of daily activities by building unit-style residences and making private rooms within the institutions, are functioning as envisioned and whether they conform to specific needs for support.

When we consider the proposition that "a smaller-scale living space is better" we have to consider it in the context of the "nature of support geared to each individual." We may see more clearly what that kind of support really means through exploring the question "What is, or what kind of place is, an institution?" "Support geared to the individual" is the antithesis of support provided in an institution; it automatically excludes an institutional environment or an institutional structure. This means that relocation to the community cannot be achieved while retaining institutional structures. That can only lead to the mini-institutionalization of community living, not to support that conforms to the users' needs or that encourages inclusion in the community. Through exploring the questions "What is an institution?" and "What is support geared to the individual?" the meaning of "rebuilding community" will automatically come into view. Community revival can only be achieved through measures aimed at freeing ourselves from institutional structures.

Notes

1) Section 1 items 1, 2, and 4 are based on the following publications, the contents of which were revised for this publication:
   Katoda, Hiroshi (2007). "2006 nendo gakkai kaiko to tenbo shogai fukushibumon" (2006 Academic Retrospective and Prospective on Social Services for the Disabled), In *Shakaifukushigaku (Japanese Journal of Social Welfare),* Vol. 48, No. 3, pp. 203-212. Japanese Society for the Study of Social Welfare.
   Katoda, Hiroshi (2008). "2007 nendo gakkai kaiko to tenbo shogai fukushibumon" (2007 Academic Retrospective and Prospective on Social Services for the Disabled). In *Shakaifukushigaku (Japanese Journal of Social Welfare),* Vol. 49, No. 3, pp. 208-218. Japanese Society for the Study of Social Welfare.

2) Onoue, Koji. Yamamoto, Hajime (2006). "Sokyu na denaoshi motomerareru 'jiritsushienho'"

(Urgent Revision Demanded for the Services and Supports for Persons with Disabilities Act). In *Kikan Fukushirodo (Welfare and Labour Quarterly).* No. 113, pp. 12-21. Gendai Shokan.

3) Okabe, Kosuke (2006). *Shogaisha jiritsu shienho to kea no jiritsu – pasonaruashisutansu to dairekuto peimento (The Services and Supports for Persons with Disabilities Act and Care Autonomy: Personal Assistance and Direct Payment).* p. 22. Akashi Shoten.

4) cf. op. cit. (Onoue, Yamamoto 2006) , p. 12.

5) Aizawa, Yoichi (2007). *Shogai to sono kazoku ga jiritsu suru toki – 'shogaisha jiritsu shienho' hihan (When the Disabled and Their Families Become Independent: A Critique of the Services and Supports for Persons with Disabilities Act).* p. 61. Sofusha.

6) Iwasaki, Shinya (2006). "Shogaisha he no jiritsu shien" (Independence Support for the Disabled). In *Shakaifukushigaku (Japanese Journal of Social Welfare),* Vol. 47 (1). pp. 91-95 (p. 94). Japanese Society for the Study of Social Welfare.

7) Sato, Hisao (2006). "Shogaisha jiritsu shien ho seitei katei de seisaku kenkyu wa do kanyo shitaka" (How did studies on policy contribute to the process of legislating the Services and Supports for Persons with Disabilities Act?). In *Shakaifukushigaku (Japanese Journal of Social Welfare),* Vol. 47 (2). pp. 49-53 (p. 49). Japanese Society for the Study of Social Welfare. 2006.

8) ibid. pp. 50-53.

9) cf. op. cit. (Okabe 2006) , p. 145.

10) Ozawa, Atsushi (2007a). "Shogaisha jiritsu shien ho ni yotte nani ga do kawattanoka" (What Changed with the Services and Supports for Persons with Disabilities Act?). In *Hattatsu shogai kenkyu (Japanese Journal on Developmental Disabilities),* Vol. 29 (3), pp. 135-137 (p. 135). 2007a.

11) Ozawa, Atsushi (2007b). "Shogaisha jiritsu shien ho ni okeru sabisu taikei no kadai to kongo no arikata – shisetsu sabisu no saihen ni shoten wo atete" (Issues in the Service System under the Services and Supports for Persons with Disabilities Act and Future Directions: Focusing on the Revision of Institutional Services). In *Hattatsu shogai kenkyu (Japanese Journal on Developmental Disabilities),* Vol. 29 (3), pp. 146-154 (p. 146). 2007b.

12) ibid. p. 148.

13) Sone, Naoki (2007). "Sodan shien, chiiki seikatsu shien jigyo, chiiki jiritsu shien kyokai" (Counseling Support, Community Living Service Business, Community Services and Supports Association). In *Hattatsu shogai kenkyu (Japanese Journal on Developmental Disabilities),* Vol. 29 (3), pp. 164-175 (p. 164). 2007.

14) Shimizu, Akihiko (2008). "Hitori hitori no sonzai no kachi – shogaisha jiritsu shienho wo koete" (The Value of Each Individual's Existence: Transcending the Services and Supports for Persons with Disabilities Act). In *Fukushi Bunka Kenkyu (Human Welfare and Culture Studies)*, Vol. 17, pp. 22-28 (p. 28). 2008.

15) cf. op. cit. (Ozawa 2007b) , p. 148.

16) cf. op. cit. (Shimizu 2008) , p. 22.

17) Masuyama, Yukari (2008). "Dareni demo ashita wa kuru" (Tomorrow Comes for Everyone). In *Fukushi Bunka Kenkyu (Human Welfare and Culture Studies)*, Vol. 17, pp. 29-39 (p. 39).

18) cf. op. cit. (Ozawa 2007b) , p. 148.

19) ibid. p. 147.

20) cf. op. cit. (Ozawa 2007b) , pp. 151-152.

21) ibid. p. 154.

22) ibid. p. 135.

23) Yamada, Takeshi (2007). "Riyosha no shiten kara mita shogaisha jiritsu shienho no kadai – kaigo hoken to no togo kara" (Issues in the Services and Supports for Persons with Disabilities Act from the Eyes of the Users: Integration with Nursing Care Insurance). *Gifu Keizai Daigaku Ronshu (Gifu Keizai University Treatises)*, Vol 41 (1), pp. 187-221. 2007.

24) Sugimoto, Tateo (2007). "Jiritsu shien iryo" (Self-Reliance Supports and Medicine). In *Hattatsu shogai kenkyu (Japanese Journal on Developmental Disabilities)*, Vol. 29 (3), pp. 138-145 (p. 138). 2007.

25) ibid. p. 143.

26) cf. op. cit. (Shimizu 2008) , p. 27.

27) ibid. p. 28.

28) cf. op. cit. (Sone 2007) , p. 175.

29) cf. op. cit. (Shimizu 2008) , p. 28.

30) cf. op. cit. (Sone 2007) , p. 165.

31) ibid. p. 174.

32) cf. op. cit. (Shimizu 2008) , p. 26.

33) Katsumata, Yukiko (2007). "Shogaisha no shotoku hosho – doko wo sutato rain to suru ka?" (Income Security for the Disabled: Where to Set the Starting Line?). In *Hattatsu shogai kenkyu (Japanese Journal on Developmental Disabilities)*, Vol. 29 (3), pp. 176-184 (p. 176).

34) ibid. p. 181.

35) ibid. p. 183.

36) Ishida, Yasunori (2008). "Shogaisha jiritsu shienho no shiko to shogaisha no seikatsu" (Enactment of the Services and Supports for Persons with Disabilities Act and the Daily Lives of the Disabled). In *Fukushi Bunka Kenkyu (Human Welfare and Culture Studies)*, Vol. 17, pp. 2-10 (p. 3).

37) Baba, Kiyoshi (2008). "Shogaisha shisetsu ni okeru shogaisha jiritsu shienho no eikyo – shukuhaku ryoko no jisshi jokyo no henka kara kangaeru" (The Effect of the Services and Supports for Persons with Disabilities Act on Residential Institutions: From the Viewpoint of Changes in Overnight Excursions). In *Fukushi Bunka Kenkyu (Human Welfare and Culture Studies)*, Vol. 17, pp. 11-23 (p. 19).

38) Sonoda, Sekiya (2008). "Fukushi genba ni okeru rekurieshon no saiteigi no kokoromi" (Attempts at Redefining Recreation in the Social Welfare Field). In *Fukushi Bunka Kenkyu (Human Welfare and Culture Studies)*, Vol. 17, pp. 62-71 (p. 70).

39) Nihon Group Home Gakkai ed (2007). *Chiiki kibangata gurup homu shien hosaku suishin jigyo kiso chosa hokokusho (Report on Basic Study on the Project to Promote Community-Based Group Home Supports)*. Nihon Group Home Gakkai.

40) Son, Ryo (2006). "Igirisu no datsushisetsuka ni mirareru chiteki shogaisha no shutaisei keisei purosesu – shuseiban gurandedo seori apurochi wo toshite" (The Process of Forming Autonomy in People with Intellectual Disabilities as Seen in Deinstitutionalization in England: Through the Revised Grounded Theory Approach). *Sosharu waku kenkyu (Social Work Studies)*. Vol. 32 (3), pp. 51-58 (p. 58). Aikawa Books.

41) Suzuki, Ryo (2008). "Chiteki shogaisha nyusho shisetsu A/B no chiiki iko ni kansuru shinzoku no taido ni tsuite no ichi kosatsu" (Some Observations on the Attitudes of Family to Relocation of People with Intellectual Disabilities to the Community from Residential Homes A & B). In *Shakaifukushigaku (Japanese Journal of Social Welfare)*, Vol. 47 (1), pp. 46-58 (pp. 55-56). Japanese Society for the Study of Social Welfare.

42) Tarui, Yasuhiko (2007). Okada, Shinichi. Shirasawa, Masakazu. "Chiteki shogaisha shisetsu shokuin ni okeru datsushisetsuka shiko no patan to enjo naiyo to no kanren" (Patterns of Thought Concerning Deinstitutionalization Among the Staff of Residential Institutions for the Intellectually Disabled and the Relationship to the Content of Support Services). *Seikatsukagaku Kenkyushi (Journal of Human Life Science Studies)*, Vol. 5, pp. 139-149 (p. 147). Osaka City University (Faculty of Human Life Science, Graduate School of Human Life Science).

43) cf. op. cit. (Son 2007), p. 83.

44) cf. op. cit. (Kishida 2008) , p. 37.
45) cf. op. cit. (Suzuki 2008) , p. 26.
46) People First Higashi Kurume (2007). *Chiteki shogaisha ga nyusho shisetsu dewa naku chiiki de kurasu tame no hon – tojisha to shiensha no tame no manyuaru (A Book for People with Intellectual Disabilities for Living in the Community Instead of in Residential Homes: A Manual for Self-Advocates and their Supporters)*, p. 4. Seikatsu Shoin.
47) cf. op. cit. (Son 2007) , p. 83.
48) ibid. p. 84.
49) cf. op. cit. (People First Higashi Kurume 2007) , p. 1.
50) ibid.
51) cf. op. cit. (Suzuki 2008) , pp. 56-57.
52) ibid. p. 66.
53) cf. op. cit. (Son 2007) , p. 66.
54) Hironiwa, Yutaka (2008). "Shogaisha no chiiki shien ni kansuru kenkyu" (Studies on Community Services for the Disabled). *Sendai Shirayuri Women's College Bulletin*, Vol. 12, pp. 51-65 (p. 64).
55) cf. op. cit. (Son 2007) , p. 66.
56) cf. op. cit. (Kishida 2008) , pp. 47-48.
57) cf. op. cit. (People First Higashi Kurume 2007) , pp. 4-5.
58) Convention on the Rights of Persons with Disabilities.
59) Quoted from Article 1 (Purpose) of the Convention on the Rights of Persons with Disabilities.
60) Quoted from January 8, 2010 edition of the Asahi Shimbun.
61) Subcommittee on Comprehensive Welfare (2011). *Shogaisha sogo fukushiho no kokkaku ni kansuru sogo fukushibukai no teigen – shinpo no seitei wo mezashite (Proposals for the Framework of the Comprehensive Welfare Act for Persons with Disabilities – Towards the Enactment of a New Law)*. August 30, 2011. The outline of the proposals presented in this book was quoted from the Disability Information Resources website at http://www.dinf.ne.jp/doc/japanese/law/promotion/m35/si02.html .
62) Fukuda, Akemi (2004). "Chiiki fukushi no jidai, tojisha no jidai" (The Age of Community Services, The Age of the Self-Advocacy). In *Shakaifukushikenkyu (Social Welfare Studies)*, Vol. 89. pp. 83-89. Tetsudo Kosaikai Foundation.
63) Mitsui, Kinuko (2006). *Teiko no Akashi watashi wa ningyo janai (Proof of Resistance: I'm*

Not a Doll). Sensyobo.
64) Sato, Kimiyo (2006). "Benchireta wo tsukete watashi rashiku ikiru" (Living as Myself with a Ventilator). In *Kikan Fukushirodo (Social Welfare and Labor Quarterly)*, Vol. 111, pp. 12-19. Gendai Shokan.
65) Mukaiyachi, Ikuyoshi (2006). *Beteru no ie kara fuku kaze (The Wind that Blows from Bethel House)*, p. 6. Word of Life.
66) ibid. pp. 186-187.
67) ibid. p. 192.
68) Nishi, Sadaharu (2006). *Sakura to sora wo kake kokoro wo tsumugu (Fly through the Sky with Sakura and Speak from the Heart)*, p. 152. Senshyobo.
69) Katoda, Hiroshi (2006). *Fukushi senshinkoku ni manabu shogaisha seisaku to tojisha sankaku (Lessons in Policies for the Disabled and Self-Advocate Participation Learned from Advanced Welfare States)*, pp. 20-24. Gendai Shokan.
70) ibid. p. 22.
71) ibid. p. 23.
72) 2003 Grant-in-Aid for Scientific Research (Comprehensive Study on Disability & Health Welfare). *Shogaisha honnin shien no arikata to chiiki seikatsu shien shisutemu ni kansuru kenkyu (Study on the Nature of Support for Persons with Disabilities and a Community Living Support System)*. (Representative researcher: H. Katoda). General Research Report. p. 76.
73) Nirje, Bengt (1969). A Scandinavian Visitor Looks at U.S. Institutions. In R. Kuger & W. Wolfensberger (eds.) : *Changing patterns in residential services for the mentally retarded*. President's Committee on Mental Retardation, Washington D. C. (Japanese from translation by H. Katoda, Y. Hashimoto, and Y. Sugita (1998). *Nomaraizeshon no genri*, p. 37. Gendai Shokan.)
74) *Institutionsavveckling — Utvecklingsstörda personers flyttning från vårdhem* (Closure of the institution – Deinstitutionalization and community living for the mentally retarded). Socialstyrelsen (1990:11)
75) Katoda, Hiroshi (1976). "Shisetsu judoji no kyoiku" (Education in the Institution for Severely Disabled Children). *Higashimurayama*, Vol. 10, pp. 8-10. Tokyo Prefectural Higashiyama Fukushien (Welfare Home). January 30, 1976.
76) Katoda, Hiroshi (1978). "Kodomotachi ni totte shisetsu de no seikatsu to ha? (sono 1)" (What is life in the institution for children? Episode 1). *Kan (Nucleus)*, Vol. 4, p. 1. Society for Considering Social services and Higashimurayama Welfare Home. November 19, 1978.

77) As far as we are aware, the following are the publications we published during the F Institution era:
  1. Kumiko Toda, Shinyo Ando, Machiko Tanaka, Mariko Kawai, Hiroshi Katoda, Atsuhiko Marumoto, Yuji Takanashi, Sachiko Kobayashi, Sakiko Kaneko, Akiyoshi Ishii, Hideki Kurokawa, Masae Kaneko, Mitsuhiro Nakamura, Kazumi Akutsu, Chidori Hara, Kazue Usuki, Haruki Saito, Kouko Haraguchi, Eiko Honda (1978). "Ensei no katsudo no ba wo hirogeru torikumi kara" (From measures to expand the spaces where disabled children can be active). (Source book pp. 43-44). The 26th Presentation of Research and Practice by Social Welfare Workers. Welfare Research Section, Guidance Department, Tokyo Public Welfare Office. March 1978.
  2. Kazumi Akutsu, Kumiko Toda, Shinyo Ando, Machiko Tanaka, Mariko Kawai, Hiroshi Katoda, Atsuhiko Marumoto, Yuji Takanashi, Sachiko Kobayashi, Sakiko Kaneko, Akiyoshi Ishii, Hideki Kurokawa, Masae Kaneko, Mitsuhiro Nakamura, Chidori Hara, Kazue Usuki, Haruki Saito, Kouko Haraguchi, Eiko Honda (1978). "Ensei ga shisetsugai no sagyosho he ikihajimete" (Residents begin attending community workshops outside the institution). (Source book pp. 45-46). The 26th Presentation of Research and Practice by Social Welfare Workers. Welfare Research Section, Guidance Department, Tokyo Public Welfare Office. March 1978.
  3. Shinyo Ando, Kazumi Akutsu, Kumiko Toda, Machiko Tanaka, Mariko Kawai, Hiroshi Katoda, Atsuhiko Marumoto, Yuji Takanashi, Sachiko Kobayashi, Sakiko Kaneko, Akiyoshi Ishii, Hideki Kurokawa, Masae Kaneko, Mitsuhiro Nakamura, Chidori Hara, Kazue Usuki, Haruki Saito, Kouko Haraguchi, Eiko Honda (1978). "Omoi chie okure no ko no shisetsu: higashimurayama fukushien no kunren shidoka de naze tokubetsu katsudo naru mono wo settei shita no ka" (Why did the training section of Higashimurayama Welfare Institution, a residential home for severely mentally retarded children, decide to set up 'special activities'?). (Source book pp. 57-58).
  4. Shinyo Ando, Kazumi Akutsu, Kumiko Toda, Machiko Tanaka, Mariko Kawai, Hiroshi Katoda, Atsuhiko Marumoto, Yuji Takanashi, Sachiko Kobayashi, Sakiko Kaneko, Akiyoshi Ishii, Masae Kaneko, Mitsuhiro Nakamura, Chidori Hara, Kazue Usuki, Haruki Saito, Kouko Haraguchi, Eiko Honda (1978). "Kizon no yogogakko, zaisekiko nado no homon wo toshite" (From visiting existing schools for the disabled, regular schools attended by the disabled, etc.). (Source book pp. 60-61). The 26th Presentation of Research and Practice by Social Welfare Workers. Welfare Research Section, Guidance Department, Tokyo Public

Welfare Office. March 1978.

5. Katoda, Hiroshi (1983). "Shisetsu bunshitsu ni tsuite – shisetsu riyosha no seikatsu no hirogari wo motomete" (About detached wards: seeking expansion of the lives of institution users). *Kenri toshite no shakaifukushi wo mezashite: shogaisha no mondai (In Pursuit of Social Services as a Human Right: Problems of Persons with Disabilities).* No. 2, pp. 118-135. Training Seminar of the Tokyo Prefectural Labor and Welfare Bureau Branch Office. June 23, 1983.

6. H. Katoda et al (1985) "Sagyoteki, rodoteki katsudo, engai katsudo: 5 nenkan no torikumi to kongo no kadai" (Work and Labor-like Activities, Activities Outside the Institution: 5 Years of Initiatives and Future Issues). The 1984 Presentation of Research and Practice by Social Welfare Workers. Welfare Research Section, Guidance Department, Tokyo Public Welfare Office. January 17, 1985.

78) N and M were invited to speak at B Institution where the author had worked. In order to ensure anonymity, not only their names but also the documents from which they are quoted have been omitted here .

79) The following website belonging to B Institution was used as a reference for current content on B Institution: http://higashimurayama-f.org/

80) The following website was used as a reference for third party assessment for social services of B Institution: Tokyo Fukushi Navigation http://www.fukushinavi.or.jp//

81) NHK Educational TV (1998). "Kurashiyasui shisetsu wo mezashite" (In Pursuit of Institutions that Are Easy to Live In). September 24, 1998, 19:20-19:50.

82) Kaetsu, Noboru (1998). "Anata ha koko de kurasemasu ka?" (Could You Live Here?). *Inclusion Japan,* No. 509, pp. 12-13 (p. 12). Inclusion Japan, July 1998.

83) ibid.

84) ibid. pp. 12-13.

85) The content of the Institution Reform Project's inception and proposals can be found in the following publication:

Takanori. Matsuo, Hiroshi. Katoda, et al. (1999). "Shisetsu de kurashiteiru hitotachi ga chiiki de goku atarimae ni kurashite ikeru yoni suru tameni" (To Allow People Living in Residential Institutions Live a Normal Life in the Community). *Shikoku Gakuin University Treatises,* Vol. 101, pp.155-174. Shikoku Gakuin University Culture Society, December 1999.

86) The following website was used as a reference for information on the disability welfare business for C Institution: http://www.wam.go.jp/

87) C Institution's website was used as a reference for the report on the protection of rights: http://tokushima-aiikukai.jp/index
88) Welfare Corporation D (2010). *Tsunobue* Welfare Corporation D bulletin, No. 332, December 20, 2010 p. 1.
89) Part of the following document was revised for 3. of this section:
    Katoda, Hiroshi (2011). "Datsushisetsuka ni miru jiritsu to chiiki seikatsu shien no jittai to kadai – D hojin ni okeru riyosha no jiritsu he no omoi wo shien shiyo to suru itonami wo yoridokoroni" (The State and Issues of Independence and Community Living Seen in Deinstitutionalization – Thoughts on the Independence of Users in Welfare Corporation D Based on the Efforts to Support). *Rikkyo shakai fukushi kenkyu (Rikkyo Social Welfare Review)*, No. 30, pp. 3-9. Rikkyo University Institute of Social Welfare.
90) cf. op. cit. (Nirje 1969. Translated by H. Katoda.) , p. 38.
91) Numbers for capacity, etc. were taken from "2010 nedo jigyo keikaku" (Business Plan for FY 2010) of the residential rehabilitation facility for the disabled run by Corporation D.
92) Numbers for capacity, etc. Were taken from "2010 nendo jigyo keikaku sakutei ni atatte" (In the Formulation of Business Plan for FY 2010) of the d isabled persons support facility run by Corporation D.
93) Welfare Corporation A (2010). *Tsunobue* Welfare Corporation D bulletin, No. 327, July 20, 2010 pp. 2-3.
94) ibid. p 3.

Chapter 4
The State of Deinstitutionalization and Community Living and Issues in Sweden and Japan
―From the Perspective of an Interview Survey of Former Institution Residents―

In Japan as in other countries, deinstitutionalization is a natural part of discussions on social services and measures towards deinstitutionalization are now evident. Some foundations have closed their residential homes. Many people with disabilities have dreamt of living in ordinary housing within the community and of interacting with local residents, their dream is gradually being realized. We must continue these efforts to fulfill the modest yet natural aspirations of former institution residents and give their dreams a form. In addition, we must take steps to address the problems of re-institutionalization, mini-institutionalization and the social structures that perpetuate the management of the disabled as a group.

Problems caused by social structures target the vulnerable and occur as a chain reaction, emerging first as admission to residential institutions against one's wishes (for the convenience of the parents or family) or admission without any room for choice. The disabled person is then confronted with the structural limitations of the residential institution itself. A further problem is the perpetuation of the atmosphere and culture of the institution within community-based services due to the fact that the residential institution provides support for community living. This structural negative chain reaction can lead to the re-institutionalization or mini-institutionalization of community living support services.

This chapter examines the effect of such problems on former institution residents who have begun living in the community, what differences occur in their quality of life, and what kind of support is needed for the future, as seen through an interview survey conducted on former institution residents in Sweden and Japan.

Section 1 Outline of the Interview Survey of Former Institution Residents in Sweden and Japan

1. Study Plan and Study Country/Area

The interview survey of former institution residents in Sweden and Japan, from preparation through to compilation of the results and observations, was conducted over a three-year period from 2008 to 2010. In 2008, I traveled to Stockholm Sweden and spent the months from April to September researching available documents and preparing for the survey. Carlslund (hereunder SC), a former residential institution located in a suburb of Stockholm and the first residential institution in Sweden to be dissolved, was selected as the study area. The study subjects were former SC residents. For survey preparations and the factual investigation, I was assisted by Kent Ericsson, who had served as the project leader for the dissolution of SC, and Patricia Ericsson, who had served as the SC general director. Patricia also conducted the interviews for the survey. SC was dissolved and closed about 20 years ago in 1988, which made it extremely difficult to find former residents. Supporters in six districts of northwest Stockholm where former residents were thought to live helped find and select subjects. The subjects were selected in the fall of 2008, and the interview survey was conducted from November 2008 to March 2009. Survey data were organized during the second year of the project from April 2009 to July 2009.

In 2009, the study area was moved to Japan. The period from April to July 2009 was spent researching documents and preparing for the survey. The institutions selected for the study were I Institution run by E Corporation in Hokkaido where deinstitutionalization is quite advanced, and J Institution run by J Corporation in the Kanto area, and the subjects were former residents of these two institutions. Survey preparations and the factual investigation were conducted with the full cooperation of both social welfare corporations, and the interview survey was conducted after hiring an experienced local female interviewer who surveyed female subjects while the author surveyed male subjects. The interview survey in P City, Hokkaido area was conducted in August 2009, and the interview survey in Q City, Kanto was conducted in September 2009. After completion of the interview survey, survey data were organized from October 2009 to March 2010. The year 2010 was spent analyzing the results of the surveys in both countries.

2. Study Subjects

Initially, I planned to interview 100 people with disabilities (50 males, 50 females) who were living in group homes and other forms of housing within the community in both Sweden and Japan. As mentioned above, however, the fact that twenty years had passed since former residents left SC in Sweden made it extremely difficult to select study subjects (the study area covered six local districts and municipalities in northwest Stockholm), and in the end only 20 former residents (8 males, 11 females) agreed to be interviewed. In Japan, 50 former residents (28 males, 22 females) of I Institution run by E Corporation and 32 former residents (14 males, 18 females) of J Institution run by J Corporation agreed to be interviewed. However, of the 20 subjects who were former residents of SC, one was 38 and the remaining 19 were over 50. I therefore decided to narrow the focus of the study to former residents over the age of 50 in both Japan and Sweden, resulting in 24 former residents of I Institution (12 males, 12 females) and 18 former residents of J Institution (6 males, 12 females). As can be seen from Table 1, no significant difference was observed in the gender of subjects from Sweden (former residents of SC) and Japan (former residents of I Institution and J Institution), from SC and I Institution, or from I Institution and J Institution. As more than half of the former institution residents had some difficulty responding to the interview, basic information concerning the subjects was confirmed separately by the staff (verbally or using the Interview Guide I for Staff Members in the appendix) or by the subjects' parents (or guardians).

Table 1 Basic Data on Former Residents in Sweden & Japan

	Sweden		Japan					
Place	6 cities in Stockholm		P City, Hokkaido Q City, Kanto					
Former institution	SC		I & J					
Year	Jan-Mar, 2009		Aug-Sep, 2009					
No. of subjects	19		42		Comparison	Flexibility	χ^2	Significant difference
Gender	8 M, 11 F	Total	18 M	24 F	SC vs. JP	df=1	0.003	†
		P City, Hokkaido	12 M	12 F	SC vs. I	df=1	0.268	†
		Q City, Kanto	6 M	12 F	I vs. J	df=1	1.168	†

Note: SC = Former residents of Carlslund, JP = Japan = I institution+J institution, I=former residents of E corporation I institution, J=former residents of J corporation J institution, M=male, F=female, †=no significant difference

3. Study Method

The Relocation and Community Living Assessment Interview Guides, which we developed from the revised Kajandi manual for estimating the quality of life, were used for this survey. The Guides use semi-structured interviews and were developed through a series of studies, including, for example, a study conducted under a Grant-in-Aid for Scientific Research and International Research from 1994 to 1996.[1] The responses were recorded with the interviewees' permission so that the subjects' own words could be retained. The tapes were then transcribed, and the data were organized and further supplemented to ensure there were no errors. First, the data were totaled and statistically analyzed for each item by country (Sweden/Japan) to determine if a significant difference occurred in gender for each item (chi-squared test). This was repeated to determine if there was a significant difference between the two countries. Next, the same analysis (test) was conducted for former residents of SC in Sweden and I Institution in Japan because the backgrounds of these two institutions were considered to be very similar. Finally, the same analysis (test) was conducted for former residents of I Institution and J Institution in Japan, which differed in the process of their establishment, etc. The use of $p<0.05$, $p<0.01$, and $p<0.001$ indicate a significant difference of 5 percent, 1 percent and 0.1 percent, respectively.

4. Ethical Considerations

In Sweden, the welfare officers in each of six municipalities (kommuner), Jarfälla, Sigtuna, Solna, Sundbyberg, Sollentuna, and Upplands Väsby, obtained permission from the subjects and their parents (or guardians) before we commenced the survey. For the surveys of the eight (4 male, 4 female) subjects who had difficulty communicating, the interviews were conducted in the presence of their parents or their guardian, such as a staff member. For the survey in Japan, the people in charge of E Corporation's E Center and J Corporation's J Center obtained permission from the subjects and their parents (or guardians) before we commenced the survey. Although we received permission to publish the names of the social welfare corporations and the residential institutions in the study results, I decided for the sake of continuity to publish only the name of the former residential home, Carlslund, in Sweden and not the names of the institutions and corporations in Japan. The names of the subjects were also concealed and I have avoided using any expressions that might reveal their identity.

Section 2 Concerning the (Former) Institutions Surveyed

Before sharing the content of the survey, let me begin by introducing the characteristics of the residential institutions surveyed and a summary of the measures they implemented for deinstitutionalization and relocation to the community.

1. Characteristics and Outline of SC Institution, Stockholm, Sweden[2]

SC was a residential home established in 1901 by a woman who worked at an asylum for children. At the time, the facility housed 8 users and was run by 4 nurses. Subsequently, Stockholm City, and later Stockholm County became involved in management of the institution and it gradually expanded in scale. By 1964, it had become a large-scale residential institution housing 522 people with intellectual disabilities. With the movement for community care in the 1970s, SC became the target of social criticism. Stockholm County appointed a working group to draft a plan of reform for the residential home, and in 1976 it was decided that the home would be closed and dissolved. A project was established to draw up a plan for closure that included the relocation of the 301 users projected to remain in the home in 1981. The plan was implemented, adjusting the conditions as it progressed, and by March 1988 SC was closed. This series of actions towards dissolution of the institution impacted the closure of institutions throughout Sweden, and the dissolution of SC became a model for the closure of other institutions in the country.

2. Characteristics and Outline of Relocation at E Corporation I Institution, Japan[3]

I Institution was established as the key residential institution of E Corporation in 1968 in P City, which has a population of about 37,000 (36,752 as of January 2011). I Institution is known throughout Japan for implementing measures for the relocation of as many as 440 residents to the community (1% of the population as of April 6, 2009). To date, close to 1,300 users have left the institution and, excluding those who were transferred to other institutions, close to 500 former residents have been relocated to the community. Of these, almost 250 were relocated within P City. When the number of the intellectually disabled who remained after graduating from schools for the disabled and who have moved in from other areas are added to this figure, close to 450 people with intellectual disabilities now live in P City. The characteristic features of I Institution's relocation efforts are three promises—"continued care even after leaving the institution," "not insisting on returning to one's parents as a general rule for relocation," and "accepting anyone whenever he or she has not managed to live in the community"—as well as "limiting new admissions to the institution" and "preparing places in the community". I Institution is currently considering further relocation measures such as dispersing the institution in the community.

3. Characteristics and Outline of Relocation at J Corporation J Institution, Japan[4]

J Corporation is a private social welfare organization (social service corporation) established in 1978 in Q City with J Institution as its headquarters. It is based on the principle of "supporting and assisting life (existence)", and it was named (J), meaning world citizen, with the "hope that humankind will transcend national boundaries, break down the wall of ethnic differences, and overcome all prejudices and inequalities to become global citizens." The corporation has four stated wishes: "to enable people with disabilities to lead a normal life"; "to perform as an 'all-rounder' in the social services field"; "to take on exciting challenges and create value in the community as we pursue our dream of a prosperous future"; and, "to think and feel as the first step in all endeavors". As an organization, J Corporation serves as a movement actively involved in fulfilling those wishes, with J Institution serving as an interim institution "seriously dedicated to human recovery, meaning the full recovery of a person's character, for each user… through operating a residential institution with a good turnover rate, actively promoting relocation measures, and employing a variety of methods aimed at liberation from disability welfare".

Section 3 Results of the Comparison of Deinstitutionalization and Community Living in Sweden and Japan

1. Characteristics of Former Institution Residents in Sweden and Japan and Results of Comparison (1)

Table 2 presents the characteristics of the basic data on the subjects from Sweden (former residents of SC) and Japan (former residents of I Institution and J Institution).

(1) Outline of Basic Data on Subjects from Sweden

The average age of the subjects from Sweden was 63.7 years (males 59.4, females 66.9) and their ages ranged from 51 to 87 years (males 51 to 67, females 55 to 87). All were single (childless). The average number of years spent in the institution was 29.5 and the average number of years spent living in the community after relocation was 22. All subjects responded that their post-relocation lifestyle (type of residence) was a group home. Some subjects (several) responded "apartment" or "an apartment inside an apartment", but after confirming the results, it was found that they lived in a modern-style group home with more family-like functions and full-time staff (or the equivalent). Accordingly, all subjects have been listed as living in group homes in the table. Concerning their educational background, more than half of the subjects had entered the institution at an early age and therefore did not receive schooling. No significant difference was observed between genders for age composition, marital status, number of years in the institution, number of years living in the community, and educational background (see Table 2 S gender ratio).

(2) Outline of Basic Data on Subjects from Japan

The average age of the subjects from Japan was 58.7 (males 58.9, females 58.6), and they ranged in age from 51 to 77 years (males 51 to 67, females 51 to 77). Three were married or cohabiting (2 males, 1 female) and the total number of children they had was four. The average number of years spent in the residential institution was 22.6, while the average number of years spent living in the community after relocation was 2.5 years. All subjects responded that their post-relocation lifestyle (type of residence) was a care home or group home. As for educational background, many had received education in special education classes (now special needs education classes) for children in the regular school or at special schools for the disabled (now schools for special needs education), and almost none of the subjects had gone on to senior high school. No significant difference was found for gender with regards to age composition, marital status, average number

Table 2 Basic Data Characteristics of Former Institution Residents in Sweden and Japan and Results of Comparison (1)

	Sweden			S gender ratio	Japan			JP gender ratio	SJP comparison
		Male	Female			Male	Female		
Age composition	50s	3	1	df=2 3.946 †	50s	13	15	df=2 0.906 †	df=2 11.252 **
	60s	5	7		60s	3	7		
	Over 70	0	3		Over 70	2	2		
Mean age	63.7 (Male 59.4, Female 66.9)				58.7 (Male 58.9, Female 58.6)				
Age range	51-87 (Male 51-67, Female 55-87)				51~77 (Male 51-76, Female 51-77)				
		Male	Female			Male	Female		
Marital status	Single	8	11	df=1 0 †	Single	16	23	df=1 0.870 †	df=1 1.427 †
	Married	0	0		Married/ cohabiting	2	1		
Children	none				4 subjects				
		Male	Female			Male	Female		
No. of years in the institution	Under 10	0	0	df=3 1.030 †	Under 10	3	5	df=3 6.676 †	df=3 12.315 **
	10 to 20	1	1		10 to 20	4	1		
	Over 20	5	9		Over 20	7	5		
	Unknown	2	1		Unknown	4	13		
Mean years	29.5				22.6				
		Male	Female			Male	Female		
No. of years in community	Under 10	0	0	df=3 1.030 †	Under 10	6	3	df=3 4.569 †	df=3 39.272 ***
	10 to 20	1	1		10 to 20	1	1		
	Over 20	5	9		Over 20	1	0		
	Unknown	2	1		Unknown	10	20		
Mean years	22				2.5 (many unknown)				
Style of residence	GH 8 males 11 females				CH & GH 18 males 24 females				
		Males	Females			Males	Females		
Education	ES:Regular	0	0	df=3 5.128 †	ES:Regular	8	11	df=3 3.752 †	df=3 13.900 **
	Special	3	7		Special	9	8		
	None	2	5		None	0	4		
	Unknown	3	0		Unknown	1	1		
	JH:Regular	0	0	df=3 5.128 †	JH:Regular	3	6	df=3 5.794 †	df=3 7.196 †
	Special	3	7		Special	9	12		
	None	2	5		None	4	5		
	Unknown	3	0		Unknown	2	1		
	SH:Regular	0	0	df=3 5.128 †	SH:Regular	0	0	df=3 2.858 †	df=3 18.335 ***
	Special	3	7		Special	3	1		
	None	2	5		None	12	21		
	Unknown	3	0		Unknown	3	2		

Note: S=Sweden, JP = Japan, df=degree of flexibility, Significant difference: ** p<0.01 *** p<0.001, no significant difference =†, ES= elementary school, JH=junior high school, SH=senior high school, Special=special support classes within the regular school or special schools for the disabled, CH&GH= care homes & group homes of years in the institution, average number of years in the community and educational background (see Table 2 JP gender ratio).

(3) Results of Comparison of Each Item of Basic Data for Subjects from Sweden and Japan

No significant difference was found between the subjects from Sweden and Japan concerning marital status or educational background (junior high school), but a significant difference did occur for age composition ($p<0.01$), number of years in the institution ($p<0.01$), number of years in the community ($p<0.001$), and educational background (elementary school $p<0.01$, senior high school $p<0.001$)(see Table 2 SJP Comparison). The characteristics of items for which a significant difference were found are outlined below.

Looking at the age composition, Japanese subjects are comparatively younger than the Swedish subjects of which the majority (63%) are in their sixties compared to the Japanese subjects of which 67% are in their fifties.

Concerning the number of years spent in the residential institution, a large majority of Swedish subjects (74%) had spent over 20 years in the institution whereas many of the Japanese subjects (40%) did not know how long they had resided there, and the number who had stayed less than 20 years (31%) was almost the same as the number who had stayed for more than 20 years (29%). As for the number of years spent living in the community post-relocation, the large majority of Swedish subjects (74%) had spent more than 20 years in the community whereas the large majority of Japanese subjects (71%) responded "unknown" to the question on how long they had lived in the community and 21% had lived there less than 10 years. The number of years spent in both the institution and in the community was longer for the Swedish subjects than for the Japanese subjects, and the results suggested a possible polarization of the Japanese subjects between those who had spent a long time in the residential institution and a short time in the community and those who had spent a comparatively short time in both the residential institution and the community. This may be the effect of differences in the nature of the two institutions being studied in Japan and in the measures for relocation to the community.

A look at the educational background of the subjects showed that whereas the majority of subjects in Sweden (53%) had attended special schools during their elementary, junior high and senior high years or had not gone to school or higher education (37%), the majority of those in Japan (45%) had attended regular schools during their elementary school years or had attended special education classes in regular schools or special schools for the disabled (40%). When they reached junior high school age, half (50%) of the Japanese subjects attended special education classes or special schools while the number attending regular school decreased (21%) and many also stopped going to school at all (21%). Only 10% of the subjects had proceeded on to a special high school for the disabled while 79% did not continue their education.

(4) Results of the Comparison between Former Residents of SC, Sweden and I Institution, Japan

As mentioned previously, the study focused on former residents of SC residential home in Sweden and I Institution and J Institution in Japan. I Institution was established in 1968 as a large scale colony modeled after SC in Sweden, and therefore, it differs markedly in character from J Institution which was established in 1978 as a transitional residence. We therefore organized the data for SC and I Institution alone in the same way as in Tables 1 and 2 and undertook statistical processing (chi-squared test). Excluding the item on number of years spent in the institution, the results were similar. Table 3 presents a comparison of the number of years in a residential institution for former residents in Sweden and Japan. When the two countries are compared, there is a significant difference ($p<0.01$), and both Swedish and Japanese subjects appeared to have spent a relatively long period of time in institutions. In fact, however, the average number of years former residents of I Institution spent in the institution was only 9.7 whereas former residents of I Institution had spent an average of 28.6 years in the institution. From this it is clear that the length of mean residence in institutions for former residents of I Institution affected the overall results. Accordingly, the length of stay in the residential institution (number of years) for former residents of SC and I Institution was compared again, and it was found that the average number of years was 29.5 and 28.6, respectively, with the majority of subjects having lived for more than 20 years in an institution. Thus no significant difference was found between the former residents of these two institutions.

Table 3 Comparison of Years in the Institution for Former Residents in Sweden and Japan

No. of years in the institution	Sweden			Japan			SJP comparison
		Males	Females		Males	Females	
	Under 10	0	0	Under 10	3	5	df=3
	10 to 20	1	1	10 to 20	4	1	12.315
	Over 20	5	9	Over 20	7	5	**
	Unknown	2	1	Unknown	4	13	
Mean years		29.5			22.6		
	SC insitution			I institution			SJP comparison
		Males	Females		Males	Females	
No. of years in the institution	Under 10	0	0	Under 10	2	2	df=3
	10 to 20	1	1	10 to 20	1	0	5.580
	Over 20	5	9	Over 20	7	5	†
	Unknown	2	1	Unknown	2	5	
Mean years		29.5			28.6		

2. Basic Data Characteristics of Former Institution Residents in Sweden and Japan and Results of Comparison (2)

Table 4 presents the basic data characteristics and comparison results (2) for subjects in Sweden (former residents of SC) and Japan (former residents of I Institution and J Institution).

(1) Thoughts about Years Spent in the Institution

As can be seen from Table 4, other than those subjects who responded that they had forgotten (11%), all the subjects from Sweden (89%) said that life in the institution was unpleasant and that they had hated it. Some subjects also showed reluctance to respond, saying "I don't want to remember life in the institution" and "I don't want to talk about it." No significant difference was observed between male and female subjects. For the Japanese subjects, on the other hand, 43% responded that "I disliked some aspects, but other aspects were enjoyable", exhibiting the feeling of fellowship that can be seen in group life in institutions and complex emotions concerning human relations. Many also answered that they had forgotten (38%). Three times as many Japanese male subjects as female subjects expressed feelings of dislike and unpleasantness towards residential live while four times as many females responded that they had "forgotten", and a significant difference ($p<0.05$) was observed between genders among the Japanese subjects. A significant difference ($p<0.001$) was also observed between the feelings of Swedish and Japanese subjects.

(2) Feelings towards Relocation in the Community

The majority of subjects in Sweden (68%) expressed happiness at being relocated to the community, whereas the most frequent response from Japanese subjects was "I forgot" (45%), followed by "I was happy" (31%) and "I was worried, anxious" (24%). While no significant difference was observed for gender for subjects from the two countries, a significant difference was observed between the two countries in their feelings towards relocation ($p<0.01$). Whereas the majority of Swedish subjects responded "I was happy", in the case of Japan, 62% of males responded "I was happy" while most females (74%) responded "I forgot".

(3) The State of Employment, Income, and Pension

As employment, income and pension conditions are closely interrelated, they have been treated here under one heading. The majority of subjects from Sweden were of advanced age (most were in their sixties with an average age of 63.7), and only 11% were working and receiving an income (as a wage subsidy). The majority (63%) attended a day activity center (hereunder DC) during the daytime, and all subjects (100%) received a basic disability pension (now sickness compensation) or old age pension with an income of over 100,000 yen/month (converted to Japanese yen). This income includes an allowance for daytime activities and for housing. No significant difference was observed for gender. This result was believed to be related to the age composition of the subjects. In comparison, many of the subjects from Japan (62%), were engaged in sheltered workshops for people with disabilities, and a significant difference was observed for gender (p<0.05). Whereas many female subjects (79%) worked at sheltered workshops, only 39% of male subjects did so, and another 39% spent the day at DCs or were unemployed. As for pensions and income, many subjects received 1st level (38%) and 2nd level (43%) basic disability pensions, with the majority (62%) having an income of between 50,000 and 100,000 Japanese yen. One in four subjects (26%) had an income

Table 4 Basic Data Characteristics of Former Institution Residents in Sweden and Japan and Results of Comparison (2)

		Sweden		S gender ratio	Japan			JP gender ratio	SJP comparison
		Males	Females			Males	Females		
Life in the institution	Dislike/unpleasant	7	10	df=2 0.057 †	Dislike/unpleasant	6	2	df=2 7.549 *	df=2 27.344 ***
	Mixed emotions	0	0		Mixed emotions	9	9		
	Forgot	1	1		Forgot	3	13		
Relocation	Anxiety/worry	3	3	df=2 0.226 †	Anxiety/worry	5	5	df=2 4.185 †	df=2 13.206 **
	Happy	5	8		Happy	8	5		
	Forgot	0	0		Forgot	5	14		
Employment	Company	0	0	df=3 3.353 †	Company	4	3	df=3 9.215 *	df=3 26.696 ***
	Sheltered workshop	2	0		Sheltered workshop	7	19		
	DC	5	7		DC	4	0		
	Unemployed	1	4		Unemployed	3	2		
Income	Over JPY 100,000:	8	11	df=3 0 †	Over JPY 100,000:	5	6	df=3 0.641 †	df=3 28.514 ***
	JPY 50,000 – 99,000	0	0		JPY 50,000 – 99,000	10	13		
	JPY 1,000-49,000	0	0		JPY 1,000-49,000	2	2		
	0	0	0		0	1	4		
Pension		8	11		Benefits, etc.	4	2	df=3 0.731 †	
	Pension/employment wage subsidy	(2	0)		Level 1	10	6		
					Level 2	6	12		
	Pension/activity/housing allowance	(6	11)		None	4	4		
Remarks	Income calculated at exchange rate of 1kr=15.8yen (as of 2014.2.10)								

Note: S=Sweden, JP= Japan, df=degree of flexibility, Significant difference: * p<0.05 ** p<0.01 *** p<0.001, no significant difference =†, DC= employment at welfare facilities for the disabled such as day activity centers exceeding 100,000 yen. No significant difference was observed for gender with regards to income or pensions. The above results showed a significant difference between Swedish and Japanese subjects for income and pensions ($p<0.001$ in both cases).

3. The State of Community Living for Former Institution Residents in Sweden and Japan (1)

As shown in Table 5, no significant difference was observed for gender in subjects from either Sweden or Japan, except for the Japanese subjects concerning the items "comfort" and "self-advocacy activities."

(1) Housing

Many of the subjects in Sweden (68%) live in group homes, and the rest (32%) live in apartments. All of them (100%) had their own room and found their housing pleasant. The living environment for people with intellectual disabilities in Sweden has changed dramatically since the mid-1980s, and 4 out of 5 of the intellectually disabled are ensured their own room in a group home, which is structured to function like a family. Therefore it was assumed that the responses of "group home" and "apartment" referred to this quality of housing. In fact, subjects who responded with "apartment" also said "an apartment within an apartment", which again is assumed to refer to the above type of housing. Almost all subjects from Japan (92%) have their own room within a group home or care home, and only a few (8%) were married or living on their own. The majority of subjects described the comfort of their residence as "good" (75%), but some (14%) expressed the desire to move to (another) apartment. The subjects are confronted with the reality that even if they wished to move, they do not have enough money to live on their own. A significant difference ($p<0.05$) was observed for gender in the Japanese subjects concerning "comfort", but this was because female subjects responded more frequently "want to move" or "unclear".

A significant difference was observed between subjects from Japan and Sweden concerning housing and comfort of housing ($p<0.01$ for both items). The difference for housing occurred because far fewer Japanese subjects lived in "apartments" than subjects

Table 5 The State of Community Living for Former Institution Residents in Sweden and Japan (1)

	Sweden			S gender ratio	Japan			JP gender ratio	SJP comparison
		Males	Females			Males	Females		
Housing	Apartment	3	3	df=1 0.226 †	Apartment	2	0	df=1 2.801 †	df=1 8.258 **
	GH	5	8		GH・CH	16	24		
	Own room	8	11		Own room	18	24	df=1	0.005 †
Comfort	Good (pleasant)	8	11	df=2 0 †	Good	15	13	df=2 4.038 *	df=2 13.532 **
	Want to move	0	0		Want to move/ mixed emotions	1	5		
	Unclear	0	0		Unclear	2	6		
Housework	Daily support	8	11	df=2 0 †	Daily support	0	0	df=2 0.012 †	df=2 61.001 ***
	Weekday support	0	0		Weekday support	14	19		
	No weekend support	0	0		No weekend support	4	5		
Neighbor relations	Good	1	1	df=2 2.515 †	Good	0	0	df=2 2.299 †	df=2 8.477 *
	Greeting only	4	9		Greeting only	11	9		
	None/unclear	3	1		None/unclear	7	15		
Leisure	CD/TV	0	0	df=2 0.004 †	CD/TV	13	22	df=2 2.850 †	df=2 37.220 ***
	Relax at home	3	4		Relax at home	2	1		
	Outings, other	5	7		Outings, other	3	1		
Human Relations (friends)	Friends/staff	8	11	df=2 0 †	Friends/staff	10	18	df=2 2.139 †	df=2 8.221 *
	None	0	0		None	4	4		
	Unclear	0	0		Unclear	4	2		
Self-advocacy activities	Self-advocacy group	0	0	df=2 0 †	Self-advocacy group	13	6	df=2 9.260 **	df=2 61.001 ***
	Doesn't attend	8	11		Doesn't attend	0	0		
	Unclear	0	0		Unclear	5	18		
Future dreams	Peace	1	0	df=6 7.105 †	Peace	0	0	df=6 9.963 †	df=6 11.522 †
	Health	0	0		Health	1	1		
	Independence	0	0		Independence	1	0		
	Travel	0	6		Travel	0	6		
	Marriage	0	0		Marriage	2	1		
	Other	1	1		Other	6	10		
	Unclear	6	4		Unclear	8	6		

Note: S=Sweden, JP= Japan , df=degree of flexibility, Significant difference: * p<0.05 ** p<0.01 *** p<0.001, no significant difference =†

in Sweden and the difference for comfort occurred because a few Japanese subjects expressed the wish to move, whereas all Swedish subjects responded that the comfort of their housing was "good".

(2) Housework

The subjects in both Sweden and Japan needed some form of assistance to perform daily housework. In Sweden, the subjects were provided with 24 hour assistance 365 days a year but in Japan the majority received support only on weekdays (79%) and 21% had no support on weekends, indicating that the system is inadequate. For this reason, although no significant difference occurred in gender for the two countries, a significant difference ($p<0.001$) was observed between the subjects of both countries.

(3) Neighbor Relations

Of the subjects 68% in Sweden as well as 48% in Japan responded that their relationships with the neighbors were limited to greetings only and the results therefore cast doubt on their relations with neighbors in the community and with society. While no significant difference was observed with regards to neighbor relations for gender in the subjects of both countries, a significant difference ($p<0.05$) was observed between the Japanese and Swedish subjects because over half the Japanese subjects (52%) responded "none" or "unclear".

(4) Leisure, Human Relations (Friends), Self-Advocacy Activities

Responses from the study subjects provided information about diverse leisure activities. This was probably the question which earned the most animated responses. Categorizing their answers, however, it became clear that most of them spent their leisure time on their own or with friends from their group home watching TV or listening to CDs. The differences in the support systems of the two countries also became clear.

No significant difference was observed for gender in the responses from Swedish subjects. A look at the results of the Swedish subjects' responses shows that many subjects (47%) spent leisure time going for outings (walks) in the neighborhood with staff members or friends from the group home. Although not as many, some (16%) also went out with a companion such as a guide helper or contact person. At the same time, still many (37%) responded that they spent their time alone. These results showed that all of the subjects' human relationships are limited to friends from the group home or DC and staff members. None of them participated in self-advocacy activities. While the Swedish subjects could not be called rich, they did receive a comparatively large pension or allowance, lived in a modern system group home with family-like functions, and could work at the DC at their own pace without worrying about wages. But as many of the subjects were elderly, they had very limited relationships with others and their situation appeared to be solitary and lonely.

The most common answer from subjects in Japan (83%) was "listening to CDs, watching TV." Although some listened to CDs or watched TV in the shared space with other people, many listened to CDs or watched TV alone in their room. Concerning human relations, the range of friendships was limited to fellow residents of the group home and staff (67%). The most frequent response to the question on participation in self-advocacy activities was "unclear" (55%), but almost half of the subjects were involved in some way in an advocacy group. The fact that more male subjects participated in advocacy groups while more female subjects responded "unclear" resulted in a significant difference for gender in the Japanese subjects ($p<0.01$).

A significant difference was observed in the responses of Swedish and Japanese subjects to questions concerning leisure, human relations (friends) and self-advocacy activities. Compared to the Swedish subjects who spent their leisure time relaxing at home and going out, the Japanese subjects spent the day listening to CDs or watching TV ($p<0.001$). Whereas all of the subjects in Sweden responded that their friends were limited to fellow residents or staff members, some subjects in Japan responded "none" or "unclear" ($p<0.05$). A significant difference was also observed between subjects in Sweden who did not participate in self-advocacy activities and subjects in Japan, half of whom did participate in such activities ($p<0.001$).

(5) Future Dreams

Many subjects, 53% in Sweden and 33% in Japan, responded "unclear" to the question about future dreams, and many Japanese subjects also responded "other" (38%). Both Swedish and Japanese subjects identified "travel" as a concrete dream, 32% and 14%, respectively. In addition, Japanese subjects answered "marriage" (7%), indicating a longing to be married. No significant difference was observed for gender in either country, or between the two countries.

4. The State of Community Living for Former Institution Residents in Sweden and Japan (2)

As can be seen from Table 6, the results of statistical processing and comparison of former residents of SC in Sweden and Institution I in Japan differed from those presented in Table 5 for housing, comfort and neighbor relations. With regards to housing and comfort, many of the subjects in Sweden (SC) and Japan (I Institution) live in group homes and the rest live in apartments. Moreover, all of the subjects have their own room and are comfortable. No significant difference was observed between the two countries. Nor was a significant difference observed between the two countries for neighbor

Table 6   The State of Community Living for Former Institution Residents in Sweden and Japan (2)

		SC (S)			I Institution (JP)		
		Males	Females		Males	Females	SJP comparison
Housing	Apartment	3	3	Apartment	2	0	df=1
	GH	5	8	GH・CH	10	12	3.787 †
Comfort	Good (pleasant)	8	11	Good	11	7	df=2
	Want to move	0	0	Want to move	1	2	5.523
	Unclear	0	0	Unclear	0	3	†
Neighbor	Good	1	1	Good	0	0	df=2
relations	Greeting only	4	9	Greeting only	9	6	3.536
	None/unclear	3	1	None/unclear	3	6	†

Note: S=Sweden, JP= Japan, df=degree of flexibility, Significant difference: * $p<0.05$ ** $p<0.01$, no significant difference =†, GH=group home, CH=care home relations. The relationships of the majority of subjects in both Sweden (SC) and Japan (I Institution) were limited to just greeting their neighbors.

Section 4 Factors that Impacted the Results of the Comparison of Deinstitutionalization and Community Living in the Two Countries

Deinstitutionalization and community living as seen through the comparative study of Japan and Sweden can be summarized in the following points.

1. Leaving the Institution to Live a Normal Live in the Community: Confirming Basic Policy

When we step aside from the traditional social welfare system that is strongly influenced by limited funding and manpower and examine more deeply the issue of what institutions are (what kind of place), we must ask ourselves this question: "What is individualized support?" The definition of a residential institution by Adolf Ratzka below indicates that institutions are the polar opposite of support geared to the individual. In his words,

> "We face an institution if
> - there is no other alternative,
> - users cannot choose who is to assist them with what functions,
> - users have to adapt their needs to the needs of the whole scheme,
> - there are written and unwritten rules which the individual user cannot influence,
> - the assistance is limited to certain hours, activities, locations (i.e., one has to live in certain houses as opposed to living anywhere),
> - the staff providing assistance is shared by several persons,
> - there is a hierarchy with the user at the bottom of the pyramid."[5]

As was demonstrated by the assessment of D Institution run by D Corporation in Chapter 3 Section 2-3, many evils are inherent to the institutional structure of residential homes for the disabled, and it is extremely difficult to eliminate the structure as well as the harmful effects. For this reason, even if the users long to leave the residential institutions and begin living as members of society, active in the community, liberated and with opportunities for change, a role to play and aspirations for the future, even if they seek an environment and relationships that give them autonomy, forging their own social relations, having their wishes respected, and being equal, the conditions established for leaving the institution are excessively high on the grounds that sufficient social welfare services cannot be provided in the community. As a result, the disabled for whom independence is difficult and who can not adapt to society have been forced to remain long-term in residential homes. This study indicated the possibility that former residents of Sweden's SC and Japan's I Institution may have been treated in the same way. In contrast, the number of years former residents spent in J Institution was far less than for residents of SC or I Institution because J Institution was established as a transitional facility and adopted measures to return users to the community as soon as possible.

For the future, we need to create a support framework that allows the disabled to live as individuals in the community based on the understanding that as long as the conditions required for daily living are met, everyone can live a normal life in the community while using social services. This aim has much in common with the ideas expressed by D Corporation: "(An important goal for us) is establishing a base in the community for daily life, including the home and the place of work or activity… treasuring the bonds with local people and supporting the disabled to live in a way that is true to who they are. For that purpose, we must focus on the user and create a user-centered framework of mutual support in the community." This will require "1. providing "small-scale living", 2. expanding the range of choice and freedom… to increase user autonomy and empower the user, 3. facilitating the user's participation in local governance activities and providing him/her a role in the community as a responsible member of society," and ensuring that "4. the place of daily activity is separate from the living place." The above represents the basic policy that must be reconfirmed.

2. Support that Makes Living in the Community Possible: Providing Suitable Living Conditions (Housing)

As stated above, "as long as the conditions required for daily living are met, everyone can live a normal life in the community while using social services." One of the first conditions must be to "provide smaller-scale living" (housing). By "smaller-scale" is meant a lifestyle without any institutional structures, or, more accurately, one which incorporates measures designed to eliminate such structures as far as possible. It is not an issue of the type of housing or the degree of exclusive possession of space. The survey showed, for example, that after relocation the majority of former SC residents lived in group homes with modern systems and family-like functions supported by full-time staff (or a near equivalent).[6] As we have seen, there are laws such as the LSS that such housing must be provided. Thus, the ideal of "equality" and the incorporation of that ideal into the legal system is what makes it possible to provide "group homes with modern systems and home-like functions." On the other hand, however, the problem of "isolation and loneliness", which has been pointed out before, occurs precisely because of the provision of such housing.

In the case of former residents of I Institution and J Institution, the study showed that many of them live in group homes or care homes that house 4 to 5 or 6 to 7 people with assistance provided by community support centers or support staff (1 or 2). Moreover, J Institution, which housed more people with severe disabilities requiring extra support compared to I Institution, undertook a variety of support measures to make life richer for former residents, involving the community by soliciting the cooperation of local citizens as guide helpers and volunteers, and establishing a group home system that allowed staff members to be on duty overnight (using backup and substitute staff). We also saw the difficult management method in which 2 staff members live with the disabled with support from staff at the residential institution.[7] These arrangements, which "seamlessly replenished support staff"[8] and consisted of "management that completely ensured the necessary number of staff"[9], were certainly a unique system not seen elsewhere. However, in Japan, where sufficient funds are not provided to welfare services for the disabled, it is likely that these measures were born from the struggle to find ways to support a lifestyle that suited each individual in the community. This is one example of the need for organizational capacity and a support network for staff members because the ability of individual staff members to support the disabled is limited.

3. Support that Makes Living in the Community Possible: Ensuring Sufficient Income for Living

In order to live an enjoyable and meaningful life in the community, it is necessary to have enough income to live on. The majority (80%) of former residents of I Institution and J Institution in Japan were working (or doing activities) during the day and received an income (wages) on which they lived. Even so, almost half of the subjects received less than 100,000 Japanese yen a month, which meant that they were forced to rely on their pensions. The lifestyle of people with intellectual disabilities in Japan generally consists of engaging in some sort of productive activity, receiving a salary and supplementing the insufficiency in their income with their pensions. Some people, however, cannot even earn this kind of income (the unemployed and those who have no income), and they struggle to sustain a life in the community (group home) through support from their families or by digging into their savings. This situation reflects the reality of Japan's social services for the disabled where there is no debate on the true meaning of a normal life and no attempt to consider means of ensuring a normal life for the disabled.

In comparison, former residents of SC in Sweden all received a pension (basic disability pension (now sickness compensation) or old age pension). Those who were employed received a pension and a wage subsidy and those engaged in daytime activities (social welfare employment) received a pension and an allowance (including an allowance for daytime activities and housing supplement). Their income amounted to over 100,000 Japanese yen a month and they were able to live without worrying much about money. This situation was made possible by the existence of Sweden's social services system which seeks to ensure that the disabled can lead the same lifestyle as other citizens, and the legal system, including such laws as the Act on Social Services and the Act concerning Support and Service for Persons with Certain Functional Impairments (hereunder LSS), which seek to provide sufficient pension subsidies for daily living and to support this system.

4. Support that Makes Living in the Community Possible: Ensuring a Place of Work or Daytime Activity

With the implementation of the Services and Supports for Persons with Disabilities Act in Japan, many workplaces for the disabled began searching for new ways to provide employment support "Many welfare institutions studied the operation of work support programs after relocation... Local governments drafted new disability social services plans that included numerical targets for such things as relocating the workplace from welfare facilities to private businesses... At the community level, the labor, education and welfare sectors worked together to explore the creation of a labor support network for the disabled,"[10] which is to be carried forward by the Comprehensive Welfare Act for Persons with Disabilities. This was a movement "towards the realization of a society in which ever more people with disabilities could work... cooperating with private companies and others to employ the disabled."[11] Without calling it an employment transfer support program, TA Institution (North) and others developed their own networks and became vigorously involved in the context of their community relocation efforts. As many as 30% of former residents are employed by private companies with high wages and are able to live a prosperous life in the community.

Working for private companies or employment transition, however, is hard for people who have difficulty taking part in productive activities. The response has been to set up vocational assistance centers, to match users with such centers, and thereby provide them with work and wages. This was the practice for I Institution and J Institution. But no matter how long or hard a person works at vocation assistance centers, he or she will never get a raise, and the reality is that "no breakthrough has been achieved in the selection of vocational skills at such centers"[12]. These problems are occurring in a context where disability pensions fail to provide sufficient income and where the disabled are not provided with daily activities that suit their capacities and interests.

In comparison to the reality in Japan, former residents of SC in Sweden, who received pensions and allowances sufficient to live on, were able to commute to places of daily activity, such as DCs, while taking into consideration their age and functional decline, and were able to engage in activities that suited them and that they wanted to do. Within this system, although work was divided into company employment, employment transition and welfare employment, the environment was such that the individual did not have to make unreasonable efforts for skill improvement. This was the environment of Sweden's welfare culture.

5. Support that Makes Living in the Community Possible: Providing Rich Leisure Time and Social Participation

We have already described the type of housing provided to former residents of SC in Sweden as well as the ample income they receive from pensions and allowances and the fact that they are ensured daytime activities (welfare employment). The study revealed, however, that precisely because they are provided with a spacious functional home, and because their right to self-determination is respected, many of them spend their time alone in their room (house) without interference from their supporters and lack connection with their neighbors. This situation results in loneliness and raises the concern that they are becoming isolated. While some used the services of a guide helper to go for walks or shopping in town, this unfortunately did not appear to solve their loneliness. To address this problem, the "contact person system" was developed. A contact person is "a means of human support that is indispensable to supporting the disabled to develop individual interests, have their own friends, and lead an individual lifestyle like other people."[13] A contact person is a (paid) volunteer who is not a staff member and whose role is to do something with the disabled. This system was first introduced as a special service by (paid) volunteers after the adoption of the Act on Special Services for the Mentally Retarded and Others in 1986, and it was established as a system after the enactment of the LSS. According to documents of Sweden's Ministry of Health and Social Affairs from October 2005.[14] Of 38,000 people with intellectual disabilities, the number using contact persons has already reached 16,660. Although using a contact person does not suddenly transform community living, it will undoubtedly broaden the disabled person's sphere of relationships and experience beyond staff members to include people around the contact person.

Were former residents of I Institution and J Institution in Japan also spending most of their free time alone, listening to CDs or watching TV? It is not that the enjoyment of solitude should be forcefully taken away. Rather, if someone can serve as a mediator to assist them to expand their circle of activity, experience and human relationships, we should be actively seeking such people. When surveying subjects in P City, Hokkaido area, I encountered about six users of a certain group home walking in two rows holding hands. At the front walked the staff person. This may be one of their daily activities for health maintenance, but it is an extension of treatment in the residential institutions and not something that is desirable in community living. In contrast, a group home in which former residents of J Institution were living held events that involved people in the community, arranged for the users to have daily individual walks with the accompaniment of a guide helper, and solicited volunteers to join in early morning walks. These measures were likely inspired by the desire of group home staff members to see the residents of the group home participate as members of the community, and this method of expanding human relationships with neighbors and the community is certainly one that will liberate residents from loneliness and help them develop new relationships. As such, it should be shared with a wide range of people involved in this field. I felt as if I was being shown what living in the community really means and it is one measure I would like to see extended to as many other group homes as possible.

Although the numbers were few, some of the users dreamed of getting married. Some people were married, some had been divorced, and some had children. Meeting these people made me wonder if such personal and intimate human relationships as falling in love, marriage and childrearing could not become more widespread. It also made me aware of a need for classes or other measures to teach people the importance of such relationships.

Notes

1) The "Relocation and Community Living Assessment Interview Guides" were developed during the following three studies and have been further revised and developed to suit the countries being surveyed and the situation of the individual subjects.

   (1) 1994-1996 Japan Society for the Promotion of Science Grant-in-Aid for Scientific Research (International Joint Study) Grant-in-Aid for the Publication of Research Results. *A Comparative Study on Quality of Life for Persons with Intellectual Disabilities in Japan and Sweden.* (Project representative: 1996 H. Katoda; 1994-1995 Y. Nakazono). February 1997. (English edition: February 2001).

   (2) 2000-2002 Japan Society for the Promotion of Science Grant-in-Aid for Scientific Research (Basic Research (B) (2)) Grant-in-Aid for the Publication of Research Results. *A Study Concerning the Relocation of People with Intellectual Disabilities from Residential Institutions to the Community.* (Project representative: H. Katoda). February 2003.

   (3) 2003-2005 Japan Society for the Promotion of Science Grant-in-Aid for Scientific Research (Basic Research (A) (2)) Grant-in-Aid for the Publication of Research Results. *A Study Concerning the Relocation of People with Disabilities from Residential Institutions to the Community.* (Project representative: H. Katoda). February 2006.

2) Ericsson, Kent. (2002). *From Institutional Life to Community Participation.* Acta Universitatis Upsaliensis: Uppsala Studies in Education 99. The statements in this section are based on pp. 15 to 32 in Chapter 1.

3) References used for this section include H. Katoda editor-in-chief (2006) *Fukushi senshinkoku ni manabu shogaisha seiseku to tojisha sankaku (Disability Policies and Participation as Learned from Advanced Welfare States),* Gendai Shokan, pp. 231-240, and PowerPoint materials produced in 2009 for E Corporation I Institution "P shi ni okeru chiiki iko no torikumi" (Measures for Relocation in P City).

4) This section is based on J Social Welfare Corporation's Business Report for FY2007 (2008, pp. 36-94). Quotations from the report are as follows: "supporting and assisting life (existence)" (p. 60), "(J) means world citizen" (p. 53), "hope that humankind will transcend national boundaries, breakdown the wall of ethnic differences, overcome all prejudices and inequalities to become global citizens" (p. 53), "for people with disabilities to lead a normal life", "to perform as 'an all-rounder' in the social services field"; "to take on exciting challenges to create value in the community as we pursue our dream of a richer future"; and, "to feel and think

about the basics" (pp. 53-54), "seriously dedicated to human recovery, that is full recovery of a person's character, for each user... through operating a residential institution with a good turnover rate, actively promoting relocation measures" (p. 55), and "employing a variety of methods aimed at liberation from disability welfare" (p. 74).

5) Adolf D. Ratzka (1986). *Independent Living and Attendant Care in Sweden: A Consumer Perspective.* World Rehabilitation Fund: New York (pp.51-52).
6) Bakk, A. and Grunewald, K. (eds.) (1993). *Omsorgsboken – En bok om människor med begåvningshandikapp* (Book for Welfare – A Book about Persons with Learning Disability). Stockholm: Liber Utbildning. The group home model mentioned on p. 241 refers to the type of home that allocates 35 to47m^2 per person each with their own private entrance, kitchen, bedroom, living room, bath and toilet. The basis for Sweden's group homes is the Stockholm model developed in the late 1970s. According to this model, the basic pattern is 6 staff members for 5 residents. Recently, 4-person group homes are being promoted.
7) cf. op. cit. (Social Welfare Corporation J, 2008), p. 82.
8) ibid.
9) ibid.
10) Shiga, Toshikazu (2007). "Aratani tanjo shita shuro iko shien jigyo to chiteki shogaisha no shuro" (A newly developed employment support program and employment of the intellectually disabled). In *Hattatsu shogai kenkyu (Japanese Journal on Developmental Disabilities)*, Vol. 29 (3), pp. 155-163 (p. 162).
11) ibid. p. 163.
12) cf. op. cit. (Social Welfare Corporation J, 2008), p. 71.
13) Andén, G. & Liljeqvist, M. (1991). *Fub-kontakt.* Nr.5. FUB. p.3.
14) http://socialstyrelsen.se/

This chapter is based on the following publication, which was revised and rewritten as needed: Katoda, Hiroshi (2011). "Datsushisetsuka chiikiseikatsu shien no nichizui hikaku ni miru jittai to kadai – moto shisetsu kyojusha he no mensetsu chosa wo yoridokoroni" (The State of and Issues in Deinstitutionalization and Community Living as Seen through a Comparison of Japan and Sweden: Based on an Interview Survey of Former Institution Residents). In *Bulletin of the College of Community and Human Services, Rikkyo University,* Vol. 30, pp. 41-51. Rikkyo University College of Community and Human Services.

Chapter 5
The Realization of the Normalization Principle and Deinstitutionalization and Community Living

In a previous study, I and my colleagues identified issues in promoting the relocation of people with disabilities in Japan and offered proposals for addressing them.[1] The issues identified were: 1. what kind of supports do people with disabilities need during relocation and what kind of support system is needed for community living; 2. what are the structural problems inherent to residential institutions; 3. what are the conditions necessary to prevent the mini-institutionalization of group homes and daytime activity spaces for independent living in the community after relocation and, in this context, what are the issues concerning supporters, systems, parents families and communities; and, 4. what are the laws, systems, policies, social values, views on human beings and ideologies that affect the process of relocation to the community. The study also indicated that there existed within each of the above topics many mutually, integrally and complexly related structural issues at the micro, mezzo and macro level. The study further suggested that to overcome these complex structural issues it would be necessary to thoroughly organize and analyze all issues involved and consider countermeasures. What then are the conclusions drawn from the current study?

Section 1   What the Study Results Revealed

Chapter 1 examined the principle of normalization, which represents the foundation of deinstitutionalization and community living. This examination confirmed that the origins of normalization and the realization of the eight features of its basic framework are important points to consider when discussing deinstitutionalization and community living. In addition, it was found that the normalization principle not only pointed out the structural problems with staff-centered group management of the disabled in isolated residential institutions, but also identified the nature of independent user-centered support and the preparation of necessary environment for this, and also helped provide a concrete image of the methods for achieving this. The discussion revealed that the normalization principle is an ideology that calls for a change in values and social transformation.

The six points identified in 1990 by Sweden's Ministry of Health and Social Affairs for dissolving residential institutions which were examined in Chapter 2 provide concrete indicators for the social transformation that will lead to a self-advocacy oriented society. These points called for a shift: 1) from the invisible to visible, 2) from isolation to being a member of society, 3) from routine work to varied work, 4) from intensive management to the dispersion of services in the community, 5) from care to social support services, and 6) from inequality to respect of the individual's wishes. Concrete steps towards the same goal were also indicated by the social and structural changes reflected in amendments to Sweden's legislative system. These included shifting 1) from discrimination to equality, 2) from institutions to the community, 3) from representative-centered social services to self-advocacy-centered social services, 4) from protection to care and further to the realization of human rights, and 5) from centralization to decentralization of social services provision. This long historical process of consolidating the legislative system and ensuring the financial resources for supports helped point the way to the kind of support services needed to make deinstitutionalization and community living possible, including the provision of diverse small-scale group homes and daily activity centers, the improvement of leisure services, etc..

Chapter 3 examined the problems and issues with the Japanese legislative system and the state of deinstitutionalization and community living and explored the reasons behind the lack of progress in these two processes in Japan. As a result, it was concluded that the Services and Supports for Persons with Disabilities Act, as well as the Comprehensive Welfare Act for Persons with Disabilities which replaced it, are discriminatory in nature. The contents categorize the amount and quality of welfare services for the disabled by the level of disability (a type of categorization by ability) and perpetuate residential institutions within which human rights are abused. The study also showed that the lifestyle of people with disabilities, which is governed by discriminatory legislation, is not geared to personal needs or desires and is in fact being supported, just barely, by people struggling to provide individualized support by taking an interest in each individual and exploring with those individuals how to create the necessary supports.

Persistent and steady efforts must continue at the level of both the individual and society. Through the comparison of deinstitutionalization and community living in Japan and Sweden presented in Chapter 4, it became clear that in order for people with disabilities to lead a normal life in the community once they leave the institution, we need to 1) confirm basic policy, 2) provide supports that make community living possible, including proper living conditions (housing), 3) ensure sufficient income to live on, and, 4) make sure that there are places of employment and daytime activity. Chapter 5, the final chapter, will highlight and elaborate some of these issues and summarize the findings in accordance with the content of Figure 1 below.

Figure 1   A Model for Building Support Networks for Deinstitutionalization and Community Living

Preparing the Necessary Environment and High Functionality for Building Community Living

Establishing individual-ized physical & psycho-logical supports	Improving the quality of life Realizing happiness		Self-advocate participation	Information that is easy to understand
		Social inclusion Full participation Rights protection Self-determination		
		Shared values between member of society and supporters		Being understood by society

Establishing legislation including laws to ensure antidiscrimination and the self-determination of support services. Building personal and organizational networks

There is a limit to what individual supporters can achieve and therefore a social support system must be systematically created to provide individualized support. This requires the social insurance of such support, in other words, the establishment of a legal framework. The foundation of this framework must be the first article of the Convention on the Rights of Persons with Disabilities (hereunder the "Rights Convention", which reads as follows:

> The purpose of the present Convention is to promote, protect and ensure the full and equal enjoyment of all human rights and fundamental freedoms by all persons with disabilities, and to promote respect for their inherent dignity...[2]

It should also be based on Article 19, which reads:

> States Parties to this Convention recognize the equal right of all persons with disabilities to live in the community, with choices equal to others, and shall take effective and appropriate measures to facilitate full enjoyment by persons with disabilities of this right and their full inclusion and participation in the community, including by ensuring that:
>
> a. Persons with disabilities have the opportunity to choose their place of residence and where and with whom they live on an equal basis with others and are not obliged to live in a particular living arrangement;
> b. Persons with disabilities have access to a range of in-home, residential and other community support services, including personal assistance necessary to support living and inclusion in the community, and to prevent isolation or segregation from the community;
> c. Community services and facilities for the general population are available on an equal basis to persons with disabilities and are responsive to their needs.[3]

From Articles 1 and 19 of the Rights Convention alone, it is clear what type of content should be included in Japanese laws. The Proposals for the Framework of the Comprehensive Welfare Act for Persons with Disabilities (hereunder Framework Proposals) mentioned in Chapter 3 Section 1 were, in fact, precisely the same as the content of the Rights Convention.

Article 19 (a) of the Rights Convention is based on the concept of community living and strongly demands the promotion of deinstitutionalization and protection from being forced to live in a particular living arrangement. Article 19 (b) demands that people with disabilities have access to community support services, including personal assistance. Article 19 (c) demands that these services not be provided on the basis of degree of disability but rather that society ensures their provision on an equal basis responsive to individual needs. All of these points were included in the Framework Proposals. Thus, the Comprehensive Welfare Act for Persons with Disabilities, which was implemented from April 1, 2013, represents a giant step backward compared to advanced welfare states. We can only hope that when the Act is reviewed three years after its enactment, the content included in the Rights Convention and called for in the Framework Proposals will be reflected, even if only to some limited extent, to make it a truly comprehensive welfare act for persons with disabilities, regardless of whether the title of the law can be changed or not.

The various (series) of studies reviewed in this book make it clear that the prerequisites for the construction of support networks for deinstitutionalization and community living are social inclusion, full participation, human rights protection, and self-determination. In addition to the above, the first requirement is the establishment of legislation, including laws to ensure antidiscrimination and the self-determination of support services, and the construction of personal and organizational networks. The second requirement is preparation of the environment and the high functionality required to build supports for community living. The third requirement is the provision of the individualized physical and psychological supports needed to live comfortably in the community. The fourth requirement is the provision of easy-to-understand information and the understanding of one's community. The fifth requirement is improving the quality of living and realizing happiness, the sixth requirement is the participation of self-advocates, and the final requirement is to share values between member of society and one's supporters.

The keys to realizing social inclusion and individualized support, however, would seem to be the personal assistance system, the adult guardianship system, and the contact person system, none of which are incorporated into the Japanese legislative system, as well as the participation of the disabled (and particularly the intellectually disabled) in policy making, a point which was included in the Basic Act for Persons with Disabilities but failed to function. In addition, we need to consider not only laws to prevent discrimination against the disabled but also laws that encompass and protect everyone who is vulnerable in society. These points will, therefore, be discussed below.

Section 2 Deinstitutionalization and Community Living to Meet Individual Needs

1. The Personal Assistance System, a Key to Deinstitutionalization and Community Living

The personal assistance system originated in the welfare states of England and Sweden, and was first introduced to Japan through a presentation by Adolf Ratzka at an international symposium entitled "Normalization Now"[4] held in Tokyo and Osaka in 1991. Ratzka's judgment of experts incorporated within the concept of personal assistance was harsh, and the impact this had on the disabled in Japan was immeasurable.[5]

In the mid-1980s, Ratzka and others active in Stockholm presented a proposal for a personal assistance system and demanded that it be instituted by the government. Conceived by Ratzka, the concept of personal assistance was that the individual user must be able to custom-design services to his or her own and unique needs... and to recruit, train, schedule, supervise, and, if necessary, fire his or her own assistants.[6] What Ratzka sought was the following:[7]

1) Not linking housing and support services into one bundle as in cluster housing (in other words, separating housing services and personal services) and providing each disabled person with necessary and sufficient personal assistance for community

living.

2) Personal assistance allowances directly paid to the consumers to enable persons with disabilities to purchase the services from whomever they choose.

It was the birth of a center-right government in Sweden in September 1991 that brought attention to this concept and helped to legislate it. The government began drawing up the Act Concerning Support and Services for Persons with Certain Functional Impairments"[8] (hereunder LSS), and a system of personal assistance was included as one of the pillars supporting reform of the welfare system for the disabled. The personal assistance system was included in Article 9 Item 2 of the LSS as follows: "help from a personal assistant or financial support for reasonable costs for such help to the extent that the need for financial support is not covered by assistance hours pursuant to the Assistance Benefit Act (1993:389)."[9]

Further points worth considering are the facts that the personal assistance system called for direct payment and that it was also applied to leisure and cultural activities. Many people with disabilities have begun using this system, employing personal assistants to enrich the quality of their lives in the community. Ratzka had the following to say about the introduction of the system:

> Direct payment is a revolution. It allows us to begin a totally different life from that of being confined to a hospital bed all day watching TV… Through direct payment we are now able to live the lives of ordinary
> citizens… We can live in the community and have a family…[10]

The LSS also declares that the personal assistance system can be applied to anyone as long as the support or approach is user-centered. For example, members of JAG, a small group that began with about 30 severely disabled people (the name comes from the initials of three Swedish words meaning "equality, assistance, solidarity")[11], use the system to receive support from personal assistants for living in the community. By effectively utilizing the personal assistance system, the quality of life for JAG members improved markedly, and JAG is now a national organization with branches throughout the country. There are also many groups of intellectually disabled people that have used the personal assistance system to start cooperatives.[12] In these groups, people with intellectual disabilities are investors and board directors, hire staff members and undertake daily work and activities. It is no exaggeration to say that conferring the right to self-determination on people with disabilities, which is the greatest feature of the LSS, changed the perspective of the disabled on "independence" and "self-determination". It is only when our understanding and the system of rules is directed towards people's happiness and self-realization (user-centered, user sovereignty, user control=the right to self-determination) that the system has meaning. For this reason, the personal assistance system, which can truly lead to independence and self-determination for the disabled, is the key to deinstitutionalization and community living, and it should therefore be applied to not just to many but to all people with disabilities. This system is one element that should certainly be incorporated within new legislation when the Services and Supports for Persons with Disabilities Act comes under review in three years time.

2. The Adult Guardianship and Contact Person Systems, Keys to Deinstitutionalization and Community Living

The contact person system is, as stated in Item 4 Article 9 of the LSS, "a means of human support that is indispensable to supporting the disabled to develop individual interests, have their own friends, and lead an individual lifestyle like other people."[13] The concept of contact persons was put into use as a system after the enactment of the LSS and differs from the adult guardianship system.

Sweden's adult guardianship system consists of two types: godman [representative guardian] and förvaltare [administrator/trustee]. The system is used when a major event happens in someone's life, as opposed to the contact person, which is one type of special service.

The differences can be readily grasped by looking at the laws on which they are based, as the differences arise from differences in the legislation on which they are founded. The god man is a status based on the special representative guardianship system of 1974 while the förvaltare is a status based on the managerial guardianship system adopted in 1988. The contact person was originally determined by the Act on Social Services enacted in 1982, but as it did not have much function, it was subsequently placed under the Act on Special Services for the Mentally Retarded and Others (hereunder the New Special Services Act) of 1986. Due to lobbying from parents' organizations and others, the system was actualized and later officially incorporated into the LSS. It has since become firmly established as a special public service.

The god man as a special representative guardian is entrusted with discretionary power for a considerable range of matters and can make decisions on behalf of the ward, but only with the adult ward's consent. The god man is appointed by the district court. The appointment is registered and recorded in the guardian's account book. There is no announcement in the official gazette. It is possible for the god man to ask for appropriate remuneration. Although it depends on how much the ward possesses, the god man can receive necessary remuneration. The district court serves as the liaison.

The förvaltare administers a ward's property and in Japanese could be translated as "administrative guardian". There are some restrictions on the förvaltare's legal capacity, and he or she must listen to the opinions of the ward's spouse, immediate relatives, relatives, etc. The förvaltare makes the final decision in consultation with the related parties. The förvaltare is also appointed by the district court but, because this position involves the handling of money, the courts must appoint someone trustworthy and in general such guardians are selected from the well-educated. The appointment of förvaltares is announced in the official gazette. The förvaltare can also ask for appropriate remuneration. The voting rights of a ward with a förvaltare cannot be taken away. The district court serves as the liaison.

The contact person was adopted as a special service after implementation of the New Special Services Act in 1986.[14] Prior to that time, it was almost unheard of. People's response when they heard the term was usually "What's that?" and the concept was not in widespread use among the disabled or related people. For this reason, people with intellectual disabilities, their parents and staff members were also unaware of it. It seemed that the service would never become firmly established, and therefore the FUB[15] (Swedish

Association for Persons with Mental Retardation) arose to do something about it. We now know that there were many people living in the community at the time who were isolated and lonely. Although they had gained their own private housing, many rarely left home to go out into the community. The desire to see them make friends, to come out and breathe the air of society, began to grow, and the public became increasingly aware that the intellectually disabled needed contact persons.

The FUB, convinced that the contact person system was an effective tool for the intellectually disabled, launched a nationwide campaign in 1991. Many people with intellectual disabilities were interviewed on the radio and appeared on TV and in the newspaper. Advertisements were run in the newspaper describing what a contact person did and urging people to take on this role. Huge posters were put up all over town. It was a magnificent sight. The campaign was carried out for about two months and was a resounding success. Some well-known actors and soccer players arose to take part, drawing even greater attention. As a result, many people volunteered to become contact persons and the system gradually began to take root. Today one out of every two persons with intellectual disabilities uses a contact person.

A contact person is like a "friend". The term seems to be imbued with the idea that this type of person can enrich the lives of disabled people living in the community. The contact person provides some form of support and assists the person with disabilities to have contact with society. Their role is to bring people who remain isolated, who shut themselves away, out into society. They can be asked to accompany the disabled during leisure activities as well. When a person with disabilities lacks confidence to out on their own, or when they are not capable of certain tasks, such as banking procedures, the contact person comes to assist in whatever way the individual needs. Their role can also be to accompany the disabled person to the amusement park, on a hike or to a concert. The contact person's function is to join people to people.

The content of activities is very diverse. Contact persons accompany the disabled when they go shopping for clothes or shoes. The disabled person can ask them for help when paying for purchases at the department store or elsewhere, or to help with communicating to the store clerk. If the disabled person is nervous about going to the doctor, if he or she needs help writing a letter, if there is some trouble in the group home where he or she lives or the day center, and he or she needs help expressing an opinion, the contact person can be asked to help. When going to a consultation somewhere, the contact person can be asked to come, too. As you can see, the contact person is used in many different ways. Alternatively, of course, the disabled person can also use the guide helper service and personal assistants.

The people with intellectual disabilities are the ones who decide if they want a contact person. They can apply for the service with advice from someone close to them or ask someone to apply for them. Because the contact person system has become well established, the social welfare office of each locality serves as the liaison for handling applications. The contact person receives a small allowance that amounts to between 10,000 and 15,000 yen. No qualifications are necessary. As long as it is someone with whom the disabled person feels comfortable and who will serve as an advisor, friend and helper, anyone can become one. The presence of a contact person would certainly expand the human relationships of people with disabilities and make their lives richer. This system should be possible to introduce to Japan as well. It may need to be more of a volunteer based measure at first but it needs to be established as a system and allowed to take root.

3. Participation of the Disabled (Particularly the Intellectually Disabled) in Policy Making

Unfortunately, even in Sweden it is extremely difficult for the intellectually disabled to participate in politics. No one with an intellectual disability has ever been elected to parliament or to a county council or municipal assembly, nor is it likely that this will ever happen. General elections are held every four years (simultaneously for national, county and municipal levels) to choose the ruling party by proportional representation, and therefore political parties must publish a list of candidates in each constituency. The percentage of unions and organizations in Sweden is extremely high, and the representatives of organizations (or other people who those organizations trust) are most commonly listed as district candidates for each party. Accordingly, it is difficult to imagine at this point that a person with intellectual disabilities would ever be listed as a candidate.

There are also very few cases in which people with intellectual disabilities participate as members of the various government councils. (A separate examination may be needed to determine the effect of the adoption of the Rights Convention.) Many of those who participate as council members are people without intellectual disabilities who represent organizations. At most, people with intellectual disabilities have only been asked to give their opinions at government hearings on new legislation (such as in 1985). However, if we extend the meaning of political participation to include exercising one's right to vote and the support measures that make this possible, then there may be aspects that can provide a reference for Japan.

Sweden is well known for its high voting rate (81.4% in 1988, 80.1% in 2002, 82% in 2006), but study results have shown that the voting rate for people with intellectual disabilities is quite low (31% in 1998).[16] In response, Sweden has been exploring how to provide official, easy-to-understand election bulletins.[17]

Although political participation of the intellectually disabled in Sweden is still inadequate, a support system that assists them to exercise their right to vote is being established. If the definition of political participation is broadened even further to include participation in the management of organizations, the possibilities for political participation on the part of the intellectually disabled greatly increase. Some examples of participation in the management of organizations are presented below.

The first example is FUB, mentioned above, and Klippan.[18] FUB has a membership of 28,000, composed primarily of people with intellectual disabilities and their parents. While the exact number is not known, about 20 to 25% of FUB members are reportedly intellectually disabled. From the 1960s to the present, FUB has exerted a major influence on the government as a lobbying group, and its members serve on many types of government councils. Currently, FUB is engaged in political activity through a disabled people's forum composed of 43 organizations. The FUB general meeting, which is held every two years and at which delegates vote on resolutions, is an important forum for determining the movement's policies. Delegates are selected through an election process and people with intellectual disabilities have become candidates, making them eligible to run for elective office. I have seen many delegates with intellectual disabilities participating actively in the general meetings. Many have also been elected at the FUB general meeting to participate as directors.

With the establishment of Klippan, a national organization for people with intellectual disabilities, in 1995, the number of delegates with intellectual disabilities active at FUB general meetings decreased, but those members were instead active delegates at Klippan general meetings. Klippan, however, is under the umbrella of FUB and therefore FUB's influence is quite strong, which makes it difficult to say that it is an independent organization in the true sense. The Klippan chairperson is the only Klippan member participating in FUB's decision-making. If, however, people with intellectual disabilities continue to participate in FUB's decision-making and operate Klippan, the major social impact of FUB could at least make it possible for the intellectually disabled active in Klippan to participate indirectly in politics with support from FUB.

One other organization is Grunden, an organization for and with people with intellectual disabilities which became independent from FUB in July 2000 and operates on its own independent funding.[19] (See Chapter 3 Section 1.) All 11 members of the board of directors have intellectual disabilities and they employ support staff and implement a variety of programs. Grunden differs fundamentally from Klippan in that sense. In Grunden, several intellectually disabled people assisted by two supporters perform the duties of a general director responsible for social service programs in the field. As such, the level of participation by the intellectually disabled in the operation of the organization is very advanced.

There are now several organizations like Grunden throughout the country, and Grunden is working on building a national organization (5 participating organizations), with the aim of being able to receive continuous public funding from Sweden's Ministry of Health and Social Affairs in three years time. If a national Grunden association is formed, it will surpass FUB and Klippan in power and will undoubtedly point the way to political participation for the intellectually disabled. Gunden members have already been participating regularly in political party debates at the local level and budget hearings, their opinions are being reflected in policies, and their influence and effect will likely increase.

4. From Disability Discrimination Law to Discrimination Law

The EU's constitution stipulates that "Charter is equal before the law. Any discrimination based on any ground such as sex, race, colour, ethnic or social origin, genetic features, language, religion or belief, political or any other opinion, membership of a national minority, property, birth, disability, age or sexual orientation shall be prohibited," and that "Everyone has the right to engage in work and to pursue a freely chosen or accepted occupation." Social insurance in Europe developed on the basis of "the social welfare model and the tradition of social solidarity that supports that model."[20] In addition, "the Amsterdam Treaty (signed in 1997; existing law: Treaty of Nice), which is the primary source of EU law, added Article 13 which empowered the EU to take appropriate measures to eradicate discrimination, including that against the disabled. A directive on a general framework for equal treatment in employment and occupation (hereunder Council Directive)[21] was proposed by the EU Committee (November 25, 1999) for the concrete realization of this anti-discrimination provision, and it was adopted within just one year by the Council of the European Union on November 27, 2000. "[22] Needless to say this development was the result of a series of actions directed at ensuring equal employment opportunities for the disabled, including various measures and recommendations within the EU. In Sweden, which already had the Act on Equality,[23] the debate arising from the Council directive gave birth to the Act on prohibition of discrimination against persons with disabilities in working life.

The Council directive[24] on the employment of the disabled adopted on November 27, 2000 was drawn up to "ban direct and indirect discrimination based on sex, race or ethnic origin, religion or belief, disability, age or sexual orientation."[25] Reflekting these contents, Sweden enacted three anti-discrimination employment laws[26] in 1999, one of which was the Act on prohibition of discrimination against persons with disabilities in working life. This act, for example, incorporates the Council Directive's definition of the concept and scope of discrimination (Article 2 & 3) and the content of the directive's "reasonable considerations" (Articles 6 to 11).

One of the features of Sweden's Act on prohibition of discrimination against persons with disabilities in working life was the establishment of the Disability Ombudsman (hereunder HO), which was defined in Article 17. The role of the HO is described in Articles 18 through 22, with additional related content in Articles 25, 26, and 31. People can appeal to an HO if they suspect any discriminatory treatment on the grounds of disability is occurring in the workplace. The role of the HO is to fight against discrimination, to work to remedy inadequacies in the statutes to ensure that people with disabilities are awarded their rights as human beings, to consider countermeasures against discrimination, and to make public the state of discrimination.[27]

In February 2006, the Commission of Inquiry on Discrimination published the results of its investigation from 2003. Within that report, it indicated its plan to propose an integrated antidiscrimination law in February 2008.[28] With the subsequent adoption of the Rights Convention (signed by Sweden on March 30, 2007) and the counsels received from Sweden's EU Commission, citing such reasons as insufficient compensation for discrimination and failure to achieve anti-discrimination targets for non-profit organizations,[29] the government of Sweden was forced to strengthen its response to the Commission of Inquiry's proposals. From this emerged the new Discrimination Act[30]. The new legislation was laid before parliament in March 2008, adopted in May of the same year and implemented from January 1, 2009.

The new discrimination act replaced all existing antidiscrimination laws, introduced two additional grounds of discrimination, namely age and transgender identity, and represented a new coordinated anti-discrimination legislation. The Act consists of six chapters, and Article 1 states that "The purpose of this Act is to combat discrimination and in other ways promote equal rights and opportunities regardless of sex, transgender identity or expression, ethnicity, religion or other belief, disability, sexual orientation or age."

The content specified in each chapter is as follows: Chapter 1: provisions to be introduced (main content: the purpose, content, and legal force of the Act, the definition of discrimination, discrimination on the grounds of sex, transgender identity or expression, ethnicity, disability, sexual orientation and age); Chapter 2 prohibition of discrimination and reprisals (main content: ban on discrimination in working life, obligation to investigate and take measures against the job harassment, information about qualifications; ban on discrimination in education, obligation to investigate and take measures against inschool harassment, information about qualifications; ban on discrimination with regard to labour market policy activities and employment services not under public contract; starting or running a business and professional recognition; membership of certain organisations: goods, services, housing, etc.; health, medical care, social services, etc.; social insurance system, unemployment insurance and financial aid for studies; ban on discrimination in national military service and civilian service: obligation to investigate and take measures against harassment; public employment; ban on reprisals); Chapter 3: active measures (main content: concerning working life, cooperation between employers and employees, goal-oriented work, working conditions, recruitment, matters of pay, gender equality plan containing an action plan for equal pay; concerning education, goal-oriented work, preventing and hindering harassment, equal treatment plan); Chapter 4 supervision system (main content: appointment of the Equality Ombudsman,, the role and duties of the Equality Ombudsman, financial penalty, ban on appeals; appointment of the Board against Discrimination, duties of the Board, processing of an application for a financial penalty, processing of an appeal against a decision to order a financial penalty, ban on appeals, imposition of a financial penalty; Higher education Appeals Board); Chapter 5 compensation and invalidity; Chapter 6 legal proceedings (main content: applicable rules, right to bring an action, burden of proof; statute of limitations; other areas of society, litigation costs, other provisions).

Chapters 2 and 3 present an outline of the antidiscrimination provisions and their content, and they include the ban on discrimination against the disabled in employment. A feature of the new Discrimination Act is the appointment of the Equality Ombudsman and the Board against discrimination presented in Chapter 4 under the system of supervision. The disability ombudsman (HO) was abolished and incorporated into the Equality Ombudsman. In addition, it must be noted that the inclusion of provisions for penalties for any violations of the law is another outstanding feature in that it reinforced the antidiscrimination measures.

The government of Sweden promoted this law as "the strongest antidiscrimination law ever seen"[31] but organizations for the disabled are critical of it, claiming that "the government's awareness of discrimination is surprisingly poor and the new Discrimination Act is vague and inadequate."[32] Nyamko Sabuni, the Minister of Integration and Gender Equality at that time, also acknowledged the Act's inadequacy, remarking that "Although we asked each local government to take sufficient steps within the allotted period, the results are still not adequate."[33] Still, the fact is that the new Discrimination Act was launched, combining the existing laws on discrimination in the workplace into a single law and transcending the limited framework of employment.

In the past, the need for self-advocacy activities for the disabled was actively debated. In the same way, the need for special provisions when receiving supports and services was debated in the formulation of laws and the legislation system (as seen in Article 9 of the LSS). Most likely, this same type of debate occurred in formulating the provisions of the Act on prohibition of discrimination against persons with disabilities in working life and the new Discrimination Act, as well as when establishing the concept of "reasonable considerations" in the EU directives, the Convention on the Rights of Persons with Disabilities, and the new Discrimination Act. This debate will undoubtedly continue in the future in the formulation of new concepts and provisions. No matter what the debate, in the end, "increased opportunities and assurance of equality of outcome" must be discussed together "as a functional fusion like the wheels of a car",[34] raising the quality of all aspects of social life, including lifestyle, education, employment, leisure and culture, so that everyone will be able to find meaning in their life. In that sense, we must continue to examine the developments following the enactment of Sweden's new Discrimination Law, which emerged in relation to the Council directive and the Rights Convention.

Notes

1) Katoda, Hiroshiet al. (2006). "Nihon de no shogaisha no chiiki iko wo sokushin saseru tame no kadai" (Issues for Promoting the Relocation of the Disabled in Japan). Final chapter, pp. 186-193. 2005 Japan Society for the Promotion of Science Grant-in-Aid for Scientific Research-Basic Research A. *A Study Concerning the Relocation of People with Disabilities*

from Residential Institutions to the Community. (Project representative: H. Katoda).
2) UN (2006). Convention on the Rights of Persons with Disabilities. Article 1.
3) Ibid. Article 19 From the above draft translation.
4) Normalization Now Symposium Executive Committee ed. (1991). *Nomaraizeshon no genzai: sekai no totasuten wa (Normalization Now: Its Destination).* Gendai Shokan.
5) This section was revised and recomposed from the following:
Katoda, Hiroshi (2012). "Pasonaru ashisutansu seido donyu ni miru jiritsu gainen – LSS to (karisho) shogaisha sogo shienho wo nento ni irete" (The Concept of Independence as Seen in the Introduction of the Personal Assistance System: Bearing in Mind the LSS (tentative name) and the Comprehensive Welfare Act for Persons with Disabilities). In *Rikkyo shakai fukushi kenkyu (Rikkyo University Social Welfare Review).* Vol. 31, pp. 5-12. Rikkyo University Institute of Social Welfare.
6) Ratzka, Adolf D. (1986). *Independent Living and Attendant Care in Sweden: A Consumer Perspective.* World Rehabilitation Fund: New York. (From the Japanese translation by H. Katoda, M. Koseki-Dahl (1991). *Sueden ni okeru jiritsu seikatsu to pasonaru ashisutansu.* Gendai Shokan, p. 68)
7) ibid.
8) SFS 1993:387 Lag om stöd och service till vissa funktionshindrade (Act concerning support and services for persons with certain functional impairments) (LSS)
9) ibid. Article 9 Item 2.
10) Words spoken by Adolf D. Ratzka on an NHK (Japan Broadcasting Corporation) program entitled "Fukushi nettowaku" (Welfare Network) on July 12, 2004.
11) Föreningen JAG (JAG=Jämlikhet Assistans Gemenskap=Equality, Assistance, Solidarity). An association established in 1992 with members who have severe physical and mental disabilities.
12) For example, Göteborgs Hunddagis (Grevegårdsvägen 210, 42161 Västra Frölinda, Göteborg) A cooperative for day care for dogs i Gothenburg.
13) Andén, G. & Liljeqvist, M. (1991). *Fub-kontakt* (Fub contact). Nr.5. FUB. p.3. 1991. This section is a revised version of the following:
Katoda, Hiroshi (2008). "Kontakuto pason to suweden no shogaisha fukushi" (Contact Person and Sweden's Disability Welfare). In *Rikkyo shakai fukushi kenkyu (Rikkyo University Social Welfare Review).* Vol. 27, pp. 3-9. Rikkyo University Institute of Social Welfare.
14) The statements concerning contact persons are quoted or paraphrased from the following:

(1) Nordström, C. & Thunved, A. (1990). *Nya sociallagen* (New social acts). PUBLICA.
(2) Bakk, A. & Grunewald, K. (1986). *Nya omsorgsboken* (A new book for welfare). ESSELTE: p.46.
(3) Everitt, A. & Grunewald, K. (1988). *Att klaga på omsorger* (Our objections to welfare problems). PUBLIKA.
(4) Grunewald, K. (1985). The Intellectually Handicapped in Sweden – New Legislation in a bid for Normalisation. *Current Sweden.* No.345.
(5) FUB (1991). *Fub-kontakt.* Nr.4. p.6.
15) Riksförbundet Utvecklingsstörda, Barn, Ungdomar och Vuxna (RFUB) (Swedish National Association for Persons with Intellectual Disability)
This began as a parents' organization but from the mid-1980s people with intellectual disabilities began to join as official members. In 1995, Klippan, an independent organization of people with disabilities (with its own board of directors and organization), was established and began its own activities while cooperating with RFUB.
This section is a revised version of the following:
Katoda, Hiroshi (2009). "Suweden ni okeru chiteki shogaisha no seiji sanka" (The Political Participation of People with Intellectual Disabilities in Sweden). *Nomaraizeshon (Normalization),* Vol. 29, 1 (330), pp. 13-15. Japanese Society for Rehabilitation of Persons with Disabilities.
16) Anette Kjellberg (2002). *Participation – Ideology and Everyday Life.* Linköping University.
17) Refer to the following website which presents an easy-to-understand election bulletin within Sweden's central election committee's homepage: http://www.val.se/lattlast/
18) For details, refer to the following:
Katoda, Hiroshi (1995). "Tojisha sanka sankaku no kadai to tenbo" (Issues and Prospects for Self-advocate Participation). Edited by the Committee for the Publication of an Essay Collection Commemorating the Retirement of Seikichi Oi. *Shogaiji kyoikugaku no tankyu (Explorations in Education for Children with Disabilities).* pp. 154-166.
19) For details, refer to the following:
H. Katoda (editor-in-chief) (2006). *Fukushi senshinkoku ni manabu shogaisha seisaku to tojisha sankaku (Disability Policies and Participation as Learned from Advanced Welfare States).* Gendai Shokan. October.
20) Hikima, Tomoko (2007). "EU chiiki no shogai ni kakawaru kintoho seisaku no fusoteki na tenkai to goriteki hairyo" (Development of Equality Laws and Policies Concerning 'Dis-

ability' in the EU Region and Reasonable Considerations). Chapter 1. In *Shogaisha koyo ni kakaru goriteki hairyo ni kansuru kenkyu: EU shokoku oyobi beikoku no doko (chosa kenkyu hokokusho No. 87) (Studies on 'Reasonable Considerations' Related to Employment of the Disabled: Trends in EU Nations and America (Study Report No. 87))*. Shogaisha shokugyo sogo senta (General Employment Center for the Disabled), p. 15. March.)

This section is a revised version of the following:

Katoda, Hiroshi (2008). "Suweden no shogaisha koyo, rodo seisaku no jittai to shinsabetsu kinshiho" (Employment of the Disabled in Sweden: The State of Labor Policies and the New Discrimination Act). *Kikan fukushi rodo (Welfare and Labor Quarterly)*, Vol. 121, pp. 50-60. Gendai Shokan.

21) ibid.

22) The above source gives a detailed account of the background to the adoption of the Council directive concerning employment of the disabled.

23) SFS 1991:433 Jämställdhetslagen (Act on equality)

24) Council Directive 2007/78/EC of November 2000 establishing a general framework for equal treatment in employment and occupation, 2000.

25) cf. op. cit. (Hikima, 2007), p. 15.

26) SFS 1999:130 Lagen om åtgärder mot diskriminering i arbetslivet på grund av etnisk tillhörighet, religion eller annan trosuppfattning (Act on prohibition of discrimination against ethnic minorities, religion and others in working life)

SFS 1999:132 Lagen om förbud mot diskriminering i arbetslivet på grund av funktionshinder (Act on prohibition of discrimination against persons with disabilities in working life)

SFS 1999:133 Lagen om förbud mot diskriminering i arbetslivet på grund av sexuell läggning (Act on prohibition of discrimination against sexual minorities in working life)

The above are the three relevant laws prohibiting discrimination in working life. Prior to their enactment there was Jämställdhetslagen (Act on equality) (1991:433), while after their enactment the following laws were also established: Lagen om likabehandling av studenter i högskolan (Act on equal study security for students at universities) (2001:1286) and Lagen om förbud mot diskriminering och annan kränkande behandling av barn och elever (Act on prohibition of discriminatory and indignity treatment for school children and pupils) (2006:67). In addition, Article 9, Chapter 16 of the Act on Crime (2006:69) also prohibits discrimination.

27) cf. op. cit. (Grunewald och Leczinsky, 2008), p. 375.

28) En sammanhållen diskrimineringstiftning (A coherent legislation on discrimination) (SOU

2006:22)
29) According to Svenska Dagbladet, January 28, 2008.
30) SFS 2008:567 Diskrimineringslag (Discrimination Act)
31) Integrations- och jämställdhetsdepartementet: Ett starkare skydd mot diskriminering (A strong prohibition act against discrimination) (prop. 2007/08:95)
32) Independent Living i Sverige (Independent Living in Sweden), *Pressmeddelande* (Press release), 2008-05-23.
33) ibid.
34) cf. op. cit. (Hikima, 2007), p. 12.

Afterword

In August 1983, I, my wife, and our two small daughters visited Sweden for the first time. There I met many people and observed a variety of institutions. At the beginning of the observation program, I met Anita Gustafsson, the head of the rehabilitation section for the Stockholm County Disability Support Department. She explained that Carlslund, a residential institution in Stockholm County, was scheduled for closure in 1988, five years time, and that the institutions of Björnkulla and Åkersberga were both scheduled to close in 20 years in 2003. Although Carlslund was not included in our tour, I was so stunned by this news that I longed to go and see it for myself to understand all the details of the process that would lead to its dissolution. My mind raced with questions. Was it really possible to close the institution? What would they do with it once it was closed? How did the debate that led to the plan for closure develop?

A few days later, we had the great good fortune of being allowed to visit Carlslund after all. It was a large residential institution situated in the suburbs of Stockholm and inhabited almost entirely by people with intellectual disabilities, just like the institutions in Japan. It was a dark and lonely place where no "ordinary" people lived—a special zone exclusively for the intellectually disabled.

As Gustafsson had foretold, Carlslund was completely closed in 1988. Kent Ericsson, the project leader who took part in this major historical work, and the staff of the northeast district support office, not only implemented the steps to closure but also undertook follow-up surveys on the residents. These surveys were carried out with painstaking thoroughness, not only to capture the historical significance and social responsibility of Carlslund's dissolution, but also because it was becoming evident that the intellectually disabled who had relocated to new community group homes in unfamiliar places had not yet been integrated into the community. Further, some day center staff members complained that the addition of severely disabled people made their work more difficult. At the same time, people noted that "many of the disabled developed dramatically" after they began living in the community, and the disabled themselves were adamant that they did not want to go back to the institution.

Swedish society strove to provide the necessary supports and systems that would make it possible for the intellectually disabled to lead a normal life. In Carlslund and its surroundings I felt I could glimpse a microcosmic view of that society as it followed this path and dealt with the gap between ideals and reality and the many contradictions.

In the end, Carlslund was closed, leaving only a few buildings, and transformed into a new town. Only the name of its founder, Krantzon, remains as one of the street names where a community group home is located.

As I penned this report, I found myself slipping back in time, recalling my initial shock 27 years ago. I pray that this study does not end as an unfulfilled dream. As various studies have shown, almost no one enters a residential facility of their own accord. The disabled themselves speak of the experience of being forced into institutions against their will and in complete disregard for their wishes as follows:

> "When I was a child, I wanted to live with my parents, but they put me in a home."
>
> "I don't remember doing anything bad, but they decided to send me to an institution."
>
> "It was like a prison; everything about our life was controlled. I wanted to go out into society but the staff wouldn't let me. They kept saying 'you can't do anything on your own.' 'Wait until you learn to do it yourself.'"[1]

These are the desires they express:

> "I wanted to go out into society."
> "I wanted to decide and do things for myself."
> "It would be better to let us make relationships with people in the community."
> "Wouldn't it be better to be freely involved in the community?"
> "Let's get out into the community."

"We'll try hard, too."[2]

Without a doubt, Sweden's forward-looking attitude as it strove to respond to the feelings of the disabled and proceeded steadily towards the dissolution of institutions and the formulation of national policies and legislation serves as a guiding presence, the goal towards which Japan must aspire. We must continue to explore concrete measures for de-institutionalization and the construction of a community living support system in Japan as we deepen our study of Sweden's historical background, including the many difficulties she overcame on this path, of the philosophical background and of the formation of the national consciousness that supported policies for the closure of residential institutions.

As I mentioned in the preface, the Great East Japan Earthquake and Tsunami occurred just as I was about to begin writing this work. Due to a variety of personal issues, the project was significantly delayed. My planned trip to Sweden which was to have consolidated the contents of this work was aborted. I could not bring myself to leave my family, friends, acquaintances, and the many people involved in social services who had been stricken by the disaster to travel far away to Sweden and not return for days and weeks. I deeply regret being unable to keep my promise to see my friends and colleagues in Sweden, particularly Patricia Ericsson, Kent Ericsson's partner and fellow researcher, and her family, and each and every one of the people I had come to know at Grunden.

I have continued to visit the disaster areas of Wakabayashi (in Sendai City), Kesennuma, Higashi Matsushima and Nobiru in my native land of Miyagi prefecture, and to have some small connection with those communities. Although these connections were fleeting, yet they drew me not to Sweden but to the disaster area. I have on hand countless materials on the disaster areas, enough to write treatises and essays on the topic, but I cannot write. I even feel that it would be wrong to do so. Yet, if I must write something to conclude this book, I feel compelled to express my deepest compassion and condolences for the countless victims of the Great East Japan Earthquake and Tsunami, and for their families, relatives, friends, acquaintances, for all those many people who are related to them in some way. At the same time, I know that the disabled, and people belonging to other minorities, lived through it all silently, wounded in body and soul, passing each dark day in anguish, enduring the burden, the suffering, the pain of living, in terrible circumstances, during the period when supplies were scarce, at shelters, in temporary housing, in new locations to which they had been evacuated, at the homes of family, friends or relatives where they had taken refuge, in the workplace, or at school. I cannot help but feel that this situation is exactly the same as that which those who are called "users" experience when they live for years on end with no hope of escape from the residential institutions to which they have been committed against their will. If we substitute the word "reconstruction" for "deinstitutionalization" and "relocation to the community", we can see that they are qualitatively the same. Disaster victims cannot wait another year, or two or five or ten. They long to be "deinstitutionalized" (de-sheltered, de-temporarily housed…), to live in the community and to receive the necessary supports that make this possible. Now! What we can do, and again it is a very small thing, is to remember. We must not forget the disaster victims; we must not forget the disaster areas. We must always keep them in our thoughts. We must walk with them. We cannot create the structures required for recovery or reconstruction without recognizing the needs of the disaster victims and disaster areas, adjusting plans to fit those needs and deepening our understanding of the issues they raise.

    Keeping the disaster victims and disaster areas in mind, I will return to the subject of deinstitutionalization and community living, the theme of this study, and draw this work to a close by summarizing the discussion. Earlier, I expressed my hope that D Corporation, in order to overcome the many issues it faces, would explore the meaning of "support geared to the individual" and would take up the challenge of creating the framework necessary to support a user-centered community, the challenge of ensuring freedom and self-determination for all, and the challenge of enhancing user involvement. To do this, we must first clarify the "spirit of support" so that we can provide supports that are truly for the disabled, supports that match their individual needs. Deinstitutionalization (relocation and community living) in Japan is still under development. The creation of a framework that will "comprehensively guarantee the support of community living for the disabled as a basic right"[3] and the approach we take as their supporters are the keys to achieving community living and rebuilding community in collaboration with the disabled. In that sense, the "spirit of support" is summed up perfectly in the following ten questions, which were compiled to help advisors evaluate their work.[4]

1. Am I really listening to what self-advocates have to say or am I imposing my point of view?
2. Do I see the real human growth and potential in self-advocates or do I see "disability" and "limitations"?
3. Have I checked out my actions and feelings with the self-advocates?
4. Are any of my actions based upon a potential conflict of interest or a need to be controlling in any way?
5. Do my actions:
   - Increase the self-respect, self-confidence, self-reliance in self-advocates and encourage them to take risks?
   - Decrease the self-advocates' dependence on me?
   - Increase self-advocates' opportunities to understand and participate in the decisions that affect their lives?
   - Teach people a process for making decisions, solving problem, and doing things on their own vs. controlling things?
   - Decrease the chances that I will be seen as a manipulator?
   - Increase self-advocates' opportunities to understand and participate in the decisions that affect their lives
   - Encourage a positive role for a diverse membership?
6. Do my actions promote respect and recognize individual growth as well as group spirit? (Lasting growth takes time).
7. Do my actions encourage and assist self-advocates in obtaining and understanding a wide variety of information and different points of view so that people can make informed decisions? Have my actions developed allies for the self-advocate's point of view?

8. Do my actions recognize that anger is okay and indeed justified in many instances and encourage people to use anger for positive personal growth and societal change?
9. Is it okay for self-advocates to:
   - Question my point of view?
   - Work me out of a joy?
   - Tell me that they don't need me and can decide on their own?
   - Give me negative feedback about what I am doing?
   - Not see me as an authority figure?
10. Do I realize that advisors as well as self-advocates and self-advocacy organizations are fallible human beings prone to making mistakes and have problems just like anyone else and any other organization?

Bifuka Nozomi Gakuen, a sheltered workshop for people with disabilities in Bifuka Town, Hokkaido no longer exists. It was completely closed in March 2010. I would like to close with some words from a 2008 PowerPoint presentation "The History of the Closure of Bifuka Nozomi Gakuen: The Starting Line Is the Community". These words have stayed in my heart because they provide a concrete picture of the approach we as supporters must manifest in the measures we take.

> When we launched the plan for closure of the institution "The Community Is the Starting Line", a five-year plan that we had refined over and over again, we began involving everyone, including Bifuka Town, the board of directors, the parents' association, the special needs high school… There was some criticism… but we were dead serious… "Don't give up. Don't stop until we've sent everyone off to live in the community."… I don't know how many times we were inspired to keep going by those words… We spent days staying up until dawn to write the application for closure so that we could relocate the all residents to the community… Five years went by, but still we didn't give up. And then it was time. Everyone was set to leave. "Make sure you don't come back!" we told them. They laughed. "Even if you begged me to, I'm never coming back."… "We will…

never, ever again, live in an institution!"[5]

In closing, I would like to express my profound gratitude to Kent and Patricia Ericsson who gave me the opportunity to undertake this study, to all those in charge of the local government near Carlslund, to chairperson I and everyone at D Corporation, to Shigeichi Kobayashi, Noriko Sasaki, Kazuhiko Takayama, and all the other representatives of each welfare corporation as well as all those working at the community living support centers and those who receive those services, and all those who offer their unstinting support to the same. These people made this study possible. I would also like to thank Akiko Awano and Miho Matamura, who assisted with the interview survey presented in Chapter 4, and to Kiyomi Kinoshita, who input the data for this book. Without their cooperation, this study could not have moved ahead and this report would never have been written. I would further like to express my appreciation to Yasuhiro Kikuchi, president of Gendai Shokan, who agreed to publish this book, and to Ritsuko Kobayashi of the Gendai Shokan editing department for her painstaking editing work.

This work was supported by KAKENHI (255177), a Grant-in-Aid for Scientific Research (Grant-in-Aid for Publication of Scientific Research Results : Scholarly Works) for 2013, Japan Society for the Promotion of Science. It is my hope that this book will provide a guide for formulating future social services for the disabled and for deinstitutionalization and community living all over the world.

February 2014
Hiroshi Katoda

Notes
1) People First Higashi Kurume (2007). *Chiteki shogaisha ga nyusho shisetsu de wa naku chiiki de kurasu tame no hon – tojisha to shiensha no tame no manyuaru (A Book for People with Intellectual Disabilities for Living in the Community Instead of in Residential Homes: A Manual for Self-Advocates and their Supporters)*, p. 4. Seikatsu Shoin.
2) ibid., p. 7.

3) Worrell, Bill (1988). *People first: advice for advisors*. Toronto: People First of Canada. pp. 80-82.
4) Disabled People International Japan Office (2011). *Warera jishin no koe (Our Own Voices)*. 5119 edition, p. 1.
5) Ishida, Tsutomu (2008). "Bifuka nozomi gakuen shisetsu kaitai no kiseki: sutato rain wa chiiki kara..." (The History of the Closure of Bifuka Nozomi Gakuen: The Starting Line Is the Community). PowerPoint materials. Bifuka Social Welfare Association. Produced in September 2008.

Appendix

Interview Guides used in the interview surveys in Sweden and Japan in Chapter 4

164 Appendix

Interview Guides used in the interview surveys in Sweden and Japan in Chapter 4

(To be filled in by staff)

Interview Guide I

Name of subject:

I **Personal Information**

• Date of birth　　　　　_____Year_____Month_____Day (_____years old)

• Gender　　　　　1　Female　　　　　2　Male

• Marital Status　　1　married/cohabiting　　2　single

• Children　　　　1　Yes Number:_____　　2　No

• Additional disabilities　_____

• Verbal comprehension ① : Understanding what others say
　1　Can understand to some degree the words others are saying
　2　Can understand the content of conversation

• Verbal comprehension ② : Ability to speak
　1　Can use some words and can understand the meaning to some extent
　2　Has a vocabulary

• Other _____

II Current Lifestyle

1 Living Conditions

1) What type of housing does the subject live in?
   1. Group home/care home: No. of persons/room _____
   2. Rented flat or own house
   3. Parents' house
   4. Other _____

2) How has the subject's housing changed, beginning from before his/her admission to the institution?

   _____ → _____ → _____ → _____ → _____

   Eg: Parents' home→hospital→institution→group home→own apartment

2 Education

1) Elementary school: 1. Regular school   2. Special needs class in regular school
   3. School for disabled children   4. Did not attend school
   5. Unknown   6. Other _____

2) Junior high school: 1. Regular school   2. Special needs class in regular school
   3. School for disabled children   4. Did not attend school
   5. Unknown   6. Other _____

3) Senior high school: 1. Regular school   2. Special needs class in regular school
   3. School for disabled children
   4. Did not attend school   5. Unknown   6. Other _____

4) Did the subject attend vocational college or university?
   1. Yes （   ）   2. No

3 Employment (Daytime Activities)

1) How does the subject spend the day?

   1. Regular employment   2. Sheltered occupation (vocational aid center, sheltered workshop)

   3. Wage subsidized employment (workplace training, wage subsidy, etc.)

   4. Day center   5. Stays at home   6. Other _____

For those who work:

2) No. of hours: ___days/week Total hours:___

3) Does the subject work with non-disabled people?

   1 Yes   2   No

4 Economy

1) Income/month _____ yen (Pension:)

2) Is the subject involved in self-advocacy activities? (Does he/she belong to an organization?)

   1. Yes (Name of organization: _____)

   2. No

   3. Unknown

Thank you for your cooperation.

Interviewee: the user

Interview Guide Ⅱ for Users Living in the Community

《Explanation of Purpose》

Eg: I came because I want to know how you have been living since you left the institution. Please help me by answering my questions.

《Ask for permission to record the interview.》

I Personal Information

(1) ○○ , where are you from?
(2) How old are you now?
(3) What kind of person do you think you are?

Ⅱ Process of Relocation

1 Do you remember how long you lived in the institution? (about)   years

2 Do you remember who told you to live in the institution? (or who decided that you would live in the institution)
   1. Parents   2. Sibling   3. Welfare office or institution staff member
   4. You   5. Other _____

3 How was life in the institution? _____

4 When did you first hear you would be moving from the institution to the community?
   1. Over 1 year before moving   2. About 6 months before moving
   3. About 1 month before moving   4. Just before moving (about 2 weeks before)

5   Who told you about moving from the institution to the community?
    1. Parents   2. Staff member   3. A fellow resident   4. Other _____

    What did they say? _____

6   How did you feel at that time
    1. happy   2. sad   3. upset   4. lonely   5. relieved
    6. cheerful   7. anxious   8. excited   9. Other

7   Did you consult anyone before the decision was made to leave the institution and move to the community?
    1. Yes   [Parent or sibling, staff member, fellow resident, friend, other _____]
    2. No

8   Who decided that you would leave the institution?
    1. Parents or sibling   2. Social welfare expert Welfare   3. You   4. Other_____

9   How did you feel when you moved?
    1. happy   2. sad   3. upset   4. lonely   5. relieved
    6. cheerful   7. anxious   8. excited   9. Other _____

10 After you moved,
    1. What was difficult?

    2. What was enjoyable (made you happy)?

    3. If you have anything else to share, please tell me.

III Current Lifestyle

1 Living Conditions

1-1 Type of Housing

1) What type of housing do you live in?
   1. Group home/care home: No. of persons/room___ No. of persons in group___
   2. Rented flat or own house
   3. Parents' house
   4. Other

2) How do you like your house (room)?

3) Do you want to continue living here?

4) Did you choose to live here yourself?

5) Or did someone else decide for you?

1-2 Furniture

1) Did you choose (or bring) any of this furniture yourself? Which ones?
   1. Chair   2. Desk   3. Dresser   4. Bookcase   5. Bed
   6. Did not bring any furniture   7. Don't know   8. Other_____

2) Where did you buy the furniture (chair, desk, dresser, bookcase, etc.) or other things in this room (house)?

3) Did you go shopping by yourself or did someone buy it for you (or help you buy it)?

4) Do you like it? Or would you like to buy a different one?

1-3 Laundry

1) Who does the laundry?
    1. Institution staff   2. Residents take turns   3. You
    4. You and the staff members take turns
    5. Don't know   6. Other _____

2) Who decided that?
    1. You   2. You and staff members in consultation   3. Staff member
    4. It's a rule   5. Don't know   6. Other_____

3) Please describe how you do the laundry.
    (If the subject is doing it him/her self)
    • Do you wish someone would help you?

    (If someone is helping the subject)
    • Do you want to do the laundry by yourself?

4) Are you satisfied with the fact that ＊＊＊ is doing the laundry?
    1. Yes   2. No (Reason: _____)

1-4 Cleaning

1) Who does the cleaning?
    1. Institution staff   2. Residents take turns   3. You with help   4. You
    5. Don't know   6. Other _____

2) Who decided that?

    1. Staff member   2. You and staff members in consultation   3. You

    4. It's a rule   5. Don't know   6. Other _____

3) Please describe how you do the cleaning.

    (If the subject is doing it him/her self)

    ・Do you wish someone would help you?

    (If someone is helping the subject)

    ・Do you want to do it by yourself?

4) Are you satisfied with the fact that ＊＊＊＊ is doing the cleaning?

    1. Yes   2. No (Reason: _____)

1-5 Cooking

1) Who does the cooking?

    1. Institution staff   2. Residents take turns   3. You with help   4. You

    5. Don't know   6. Other _____

2) Who decided that?

    1. Staff member   2. You and staff members in consultation   3. You

    4. It's a rule   5. Don't know   6. Other _____

3) Please describe how you do the cooking.

    (If the subject is doing it him/her self)

    ・Do you wish someone would help you?

    (If someone is helping the subject)

    ・Do you want to do it by yourself?

4) Are you satisfied with the fact that ＊＊＊＊ is doing the cooking?
   1. Yes   2. No (Reason: _____)

1-6 Shopping

1) Who does the shopping
   1. Institution staff   2. Residents take turns   3. You with help   4. You
   5. Don't know   6. Other _____

2) Who decided that?
   1. Staff member   2. You and staff members in consultation   3. You
   4. It's a rule   5. Don't know   6. Other

3) Please describe how you do the shopping.
   (If the subject is doing it him/her self)
   • Do you wish someone would help you?

   (If someone is helping the subject)
   • Do you want to do it by yourself?

4) Are you satisfied with the fact that ＊＊＊＊ is doing the shopping?
   1. Yes   2. No (Reason: _____)

1-7 Relationships

1) Do you get along with your neighbors (people in the community)?
   1. Greetings only   2. Have tea together   3. Go out together
   4. No relationship   5. Don't know   6. Other _____

2) Are you satisfied with your relationship with your neighbors?

   1. Yes   2. No (Reason:)

2   Education

  1) Did you go to elementary school?

    1. Regular school   2. Special needs class in regular school

    3. School for disabled children

    4. Did not attend school   5. Unknown   6. Other_____

  2) Did you go to junior high school?

    1. Regular school   2. Special needs class in regular school

    3. School for disabled children

    4. Did not attend school   5. Unknown   6. Other _____

  3) Did you go to senior high school?

    1. Regular school   2. Special needs class in regular school

    3. School for disabled children

    4. Did not attend school   5. Unknown   6. Other _____

  4) Did you attend vocational college or university?

  5) How did you like school? Please tell me anything you remember about school.

  6) Is there anything you want to study more? (For example, computers, gardening, how to take a video, etc.)

3 Employment (Daytime Activities)

1) How do you spend your day?
   1. Regular employment
   2. Sheltered occupation (vocational aid center, sheltered workshop)
   3. Wage subsidized employment (workplace training, wage subsidy, etc.)
   4. Day center
   5. Stay at home
   6. Other _____

2) Please tell me what you do there.

3) Who decided that you would do that activity?
   1. Staff member   2. You and the staff members in consultation   3. You
   4. Don't know   5. Other _____

(If the subject is employed)
4) No. of hours/day: ____ Hours/week: ____

5) Where is your workplace?

6) Why did you start working there?

7) Did you decide to take that job yourself?

8) What kind of work do you do?

9) Do you like it?

10) Do you want to continue doing that job for a long time?

11) Do you get along well with your coworkers or not?

(If not, why not?)

12) Do you want to work in a different place?

(If yes) Do you think that will be possible?

13) Have you ever changed jobs before? (dismissed or transferred)

14) Did someone help you find another job?

15) Who?

16) Do you feel like your hopes for the future are gradually being realized?

17) Are you satisfied with the way you spend your day?
    1. Yes   2. No (Reason:)

4 Economy

1) How much money do you receive per month?_____

2) Do you think you are receiving a lot? Or do you think it is not so much? Why do you think so?

3) Do you think the amount of money is right for the job you do?

4) How much pension do you get?

5) Do you think your income (pension, wages, etc. combined) is a lot or do you think it is not so much?

6) How much is your monthly allowance?

7) Do you think your allowance is a lot or not so much? Why do you think so?

8) What do you use your allowance for?

9) Who manages your bank books?
   1. You   2. Staff member   3. Parents, sibling   4. Guardian   5. Don't know
   6. Other_____

10) Are you able to manage your money and your bank book by yourself or do you ask someone to help you?
   1. You   2. Staff member   3. Parents, sibling   4. Guardian   5. Don't know
   6. Other_____

   (If the subject is managing it)
   • Does it make you happy and do you enjoy managing your money/bank book on your own?
   • Do you ever wish someone would help you? Do you feel anxious about doing it?

   (If someone is helping the subject)
   • What do you think about that? Do you want to manage it yourself? Do you think that you could?
   • Are you able to tell someone what you think?

11) Have you ever been to the bank or the post office?

12) Can you withdraw or deposit money at the bank or post office yourself or do you need someone to help you?

(If the subject can do it)
• Does it make you happy to do it yourself? Do you ever wish someone would help you? Do you feel anxious about doing it?

(If someone is helping the subject)
• What do you think about that? Do you want to do it yourself? Do you think that you could? What do you think you need to do to make it possible?

13) Do you have any worries about money for the future?

5 Leisure

1) What do you do in your free time?

1. Go for a walk	Often	Sometimes	Seldom	Never
2. Go for a drive	Often	Sometimes	Seldom	Never
3. Bike/motorbike	Often	Sometimes	Seldom	Never
4. Eat out	Often	Sometimes	Seldom	Never
5. Movies	Often	Sometimes	Seldom	Never
6. Art	Often	Sometimes	Seldom	Never
7. Music	Often	Sometimes	Seldom	Never
8. Church	Often	Sometimes	Seldom	Never
9. Party	Often	Sometimes	Seldom	Never
10. Sports	Often	Sometimes	Seldom	Never

What kind of sports?_____

11. Travel	Often	Sometimes	Seldom	Never
12. Other (karaoke, pachinko)	Often	Sometimes	Seldom	Never

2) If you did not have this interview today, what do you think would you be doing now?

3) Do you always do that?

4) When you go out in your spare time (or during other activities) do you go alone or does someone go with you?
(If the subject goes alone)
- Is it fun to go out on your own? Why?
- Do you wish you could go with someone?

(If the subject goes out with another person)
- Who do you go with? Is it fun?
- Are you able to tell them what you think?

5) When you go out, how do you get to where you want to go? (on foot, by bicycle, by bus, taxi or car)

6) What do you think about that? Would you like to go a different way? Do you think that is possible?

7) When you are at home in the evening or on the weekends (Saturday or Sunday), are you always on your own or do you spend time with someone else?
(If the subject spends time alone)
- Do you enjoy being on your own? Why?

- Do you want to be with other people?

(If with others)
- Who do you spend your time with? Do you enjioy being with them? Why?

- Do you want to spend your time with someone else? Who? Why?

8) Do you go to visit someone else's house?
(If yes)
- Whose house do you go to? What do you do there? Is it fun?

(If no)
- Do you want to go to someone's house? Do you think that is possible?

9) Do you drink alcohol?

10) What do you drink? (beer, sake, wine, whiskey, etc.)

11) Who do you drink with? When? What type of occasion? Where? Is it fun?

12) When you are not working and have free time, what do you want to do?

13) Do you like to play?

14) What do you enjoy playing the most?

6 Personal Relationships

1) Do you have any friends?
   1. Yes   2. No   3. Don't know   4. Other

2) If yes, who are they?
   1. Former co-resident from institution   2. Coworker   3. Staff member
   4. Mother   5. Father   6. Sibling   7. Neighbor   8. Don't know
   9. Other _____

3) What do you do with your friends?
   1. Go out together   2. Write letters   3. Watch TV
   4. Talk about things that bother us   5. Don't know   6. Other_____

4) Do you want more friends?
   1. Yes   2. No   3. Don't know

5) How often do you want to meet your friends?
   1. Frequently (more often)   2. Not so often (less often)   3. As much as now

(If the subject has friends)
- What do you do when you are together?

- Is it fun? What do you enjoy doing?

- How long have you been friends? About how many years?

- Do you want to continue being friends for many years?

- Is there anything you don't like about being with your friends? What?

(If the subject does not have friends)
- Do you want a friend or not?

- Do you think you can make a friend? Why do you think so?

6) Do you have a boyfriend/girlfriend?
   1. Yes   2. No

   (If yes)
   • Do you have enough chances to be together alone?
      1. Yes   2. Not enough   3. None at all

   • What do you do when you are together?

   (If no)
   • Do you want a boyfriend/girlfriend?

   • Do you not want a boyfriend/girlfriend? Why not?

7) Do you ever feel lonely or anxious?
   (If yes)
   • When do you feel that way?

   • What do you do when you feel that way?

   • Is there anyone who comforts you or who will give you advice?

   (If no)
   • Who? How do they comfort or advise you?

8) Do you ever comfort or give advice to others?
   (If yes)
   • Who? What do you do?

9) Have you ever wanted to get married to someone? Do you want to get married in the future?
   1. Yes   2. No   3. Don't know   4. Other_____

10) Have you ever wanted to have children? Do you want to have children in the future?
    1. Yes   2. No   3. Don't know   4. Other_____

7 Participation in Policy Making

1) Have you ever participated in an election?
   1. Yes   2. No   3. Don't know

2) Have you ever participated in meetings or discussions?
   What kind of meetings?
   1. No   2. Self-advocacy meetings for the disabled
   3. Discussions held by the organization providing services
   4. Don't know   5. Other_____

   (If participating)
   • Do you think it is better to participate with friends than on your own?

   • What do you do at these meetings?

   • Can you share your opinions at the meetings?

   • Who recommended that you participate?

   • Do you enjoy participating?

(If not participating)
- Why not? Would you like to participate in some activity like that?

8   Future Ambitions

   1) Is there anything that you feel very strongly you want to do in the future?
      1. Yes. (Specifically) _____
      2. No

9   Is there anything that you would like to ask me before we finish the interview?

Thank you very much for your help.